Janis Ian
SONGBOOK

This songbook is dedicated to
Sis Cunningham & Gordon Friesen, publishers of *Broadside Magazine*,
who were the first to publish me, present me, and give me a platform for my work.

Thank you forever.

Janis

Project Manager: Aaron Stang
Transcribed by: Janis Ian and Hemme Luttjeboer
Music Editor: Aaron Stang and Colgan Bryan
Cover Photo Courtesy of Beth Gwinn
Book Layout: Ken Rehm

WARNER BROS. PUBLICATIONS - THE GLOBAL LEADER IN PRINT
USA: 15800 NW 48th Avenue, Miami, FL 33014

WARNER/CHAPPELL MUSIC
CANADA: 85 SCARSDALE ROAD, SUITE 101
DON MILLS, ONTARIO, M3B 2R2
SCANDINAVIA: P.O. BOX 533, VENDEVAGEN 85 B
S-182 15, DANDERYD, SWEDEN
AUSTRALIA: P.O. BOX 353
3 TALAVERA ROAD, NORTH RYDE N.S.W. 2113

NUOVA CARISCH
ITALY: VIA M.F. QUINTILIANO 40
20138 MILANO
SPAIN: MAGALLANES, 25
28015 MADRID

INTERNATIONAL MUSIC PUBLICATIONS LIMITED
ENGLAND: SOUTHEND ROAD,
WOODFORD GREEN, ESSEX IG8 8HN
FRANCE: 25 RUE D'HAUTEVILLE, 75010 PARIS
GERMANY: MARSTALLSTR. 8, D-80539 MUNCHEN
DENMARK: DANMUSIK, VOGNMAGERGADE 7
DK 1120 KOBENHAVNK

CW00594445

Janis Ian's prized Martin guitar, serial # 67053, has been missing since 1973.
If you have any information, please contact her at P.O. Box 121797, Nashville, TN 37212

Thank You

Contents

Janis Ian:
A Life In Music

Janis Ian endures as one of the most important composer-performers of our time. Equally gifted as an instrumentalist, a singer and a songwriter, she has outlasted virtually all her contemporaries as a modern music force.

Ian's gift is her diversity. She is capable of extraordinary social commentary songs. Her keenly observed lyrics can tell the most remarkable narratives. And she also remains the most tender, empathetic and thoughtful of love-song writers. Illustrating her wide span as a composer is the fact that Janis Ian's creations have been recorded by everyone from Stan Getz to Dottie West, from Hugh Masekela to Vanilla Fudge, from Joan Baez to Etta James.

The woman who gave us Roberta Flack's "Jesse," Bette Midler's "Some People's Lives" and Amy Grant's "What About the Love" was also the teen protest singer of "Society's Child," the sensitive wallflower of "At Seventeen" and the disco queen of "Fly Too High."

Thirty years after she emerged as a child prodigy in a hippie world scented with incense, tear gas and cannabis, Janis Ian is writing and singing songs as powerfully as ever. Almost alone among her contemporaries Janis Ian has found a way to translate her extraordinary gifts into every era of modern American popular song. She stands unique as a talent who has received Grammy Award nominations in the '60s, the '70s, the '80s and the '90s.

"A number of my contemporaries don't have the 'hunger' to create any more," she observes. "I've always just marched on and made my living. I'm a writer and a performer. That's what I do. I have never been 'hip.' I was lucky to have gotten in the door when I did, at such a creative time. But I've never allowed myself to become bitter when times changed. I can't afford that; besides, I believe that bitterness kills art. That's probably why I still have my hunger, my creative drive."

Born in 1951, Janis Ian burst on the scene at age 15 with her controversial saga of interracial love "Society's Child." Her debut album, 1967's **Janis Ian,** garnered her the first of her nine Grammy nominations to date. Since then, there have been 15 albums of her songs. Ian is unusual in that she has never recorded a song that she did not write.

She achieved a new level of popularity in the 1970s with her trio of masterpieces **Stars** (1973), **Between the Lines** (1975) and **Aftertones** (1976). The first contained "Jesse," which became a pop standard after Roberta Flack topped the charts with it, as well as the deeply insightful "Stars," which has been recorded by talents as disparate as Glen Campbell and Cher. The second contained "At Seventeen," which sold a million copies and earned Ian her first Grammy Award. The third was one of the most critically acclaimed albums of its day and featured Ian's friends Odetta and Phoebe Snow as supporting vocalists. It spawned a No.1 hit in Japan, "Love Is Blind."

Janis Ian entered the '80s with her album **Night Rains.** It included "The Other Side of the Sun," which became a hit in Britain, as well as the international disco favorite "Fly Too High." The latter was featured on the soundtrack of the Jodie Foster movie **Foxes.** This was one of several film-music ventures for her — Ian has either scored or contributed title tunes to such movies as **Virus** (1980), **Betrayal** (1977), **The Bell Jar** (1979) and **Four Rode Out** (1969). She has also contributed to such television projects as the ABC Movie of the Week **"Freedom"** (1981) and the hit series **"Murder She Wrote"** (1987).

She won her second Grammy Award for children's music because of her work on the 1982 album **In Harmony 2.** The Recording Academy has also recognized her as a jazz artist by nominating her for a 1981 "Best vocal, duo or group" Grammy with Mel Torme. The song was her composition "Silly Habits." Janis Ian has also studied acting (with Stella Adler), directing, scoring and ballet,"though I was miserably bad at the ballet part."

People who come to see Janis Ian for the first time usually know none of this. Perhaps they know only a voice and a song or two. They invariably leave her shows stunned by her lead instrumental work on piano and guitar, as well as by the depth of her composing talent.

"I get told a lot, 'You play like a guy,' and I'm not quite sure I know what that means. I guess it's meant to be a compliment. I do know that back when I started, women just didn't play. They might strum along and accompany themselves, but they weren't players. So when people see me live for the first time, it's always this big surprise to them."

In the truest sense of the word, she is a "musician's musician." During her career she has swapped instrumental licks with everyone from rocker Jimi Hendrix to jazz pianist Chick Corea to guitarist Chet Atkins. She was among the players chosen to salute the legendary Atkins at an all-star gala in 1997 that included Dire Straits leader Mark Knopfler, jazz star Larry Carlton, bluegrass patriarch Earl Scruggs, King Crimson's Adrian Belew, pop icon Pat Boone, and country headliners Travis Tritt and Clint Black.

The 1990s have been a decade of intense creative renewal for Janis Ian. During the late 1980s she was beset by severe health and financial problems. The New Jersey native had spent most of her career in Philadelphia, New York, and Los Angeles, but in 1988 she relocated to Nashville to connect with the city's renowned songwriting and instrumental communities. Since then she has reached out to a whole new generation of listeners.

Rock star John Mellencamp brought her back on disc after a decade of silence on the soundtrack of his 1992 film *Falling From Grace.* She contributed "Days Like These" to the project. Mellencamp subsequently recorded Ian's "All Roads to the River," and issued it as a single and video from his million-selling *Human Wheels* recording. Folk star Nanci Griffith sang Janis Ian's "This Old Town" on her Grammy winning album *Other Voices Other Rooms.*

In 1993 Janis returned with a full collection of new material, *Breaking Silence*. It included her own version of "All Roads to the River," as well as such outstanding songs as "This Train Still Runs," "Ride Me Like a Wave" and her powerful Holocaust reflection "Tattoo." Two of the album's songs were given wide exposure by superstars. Amy Grant sang the collection's "What About the Love" on her million-selling album *Lead Me On*. And Bette Midler used "Some People's Lives" as the title tune for a two million-selling CD. *Breaking Silence* was nominated for a Grammy Award as Contemporary Folk Album of the Year.

Further illustrating her diversity as a songsmith, Janis Ian wrote a Christmas gem. Kathy Mattea recorded Ian's "Emmanuel" on her Grammy-winning 1994 album *Good News.* The number was revived by Ian, Mattea and Deana Carter in 1997 *for the Windham Hill release, Carols of Christmas.*

In 1995 came the Janis Ian collection *Revenge,* nominated as Pop Album of the Year at the Nashville Music Awards. Among its standout songs were "Take No Prisoners," "Ruby" and the profoundly moving "When Angels Cry."

Janis signed with the prestigious Windham Hill Records in 1997. Her debut for the company was the stunning collection *Hunger*, featuring the incisive social commentary lyric "Searching for America," her wry observation of life as a folk troubadour "Welcome to Acousticville" and one of her loveliest heartache songs, "Getting Over You."

Hunger is the work of a woman whose talent has already carried her through one of the most impressive and varied entertainment careers of our time. And it's a career that shows no signs of slowing down. Janis Ian remains one of popular music's most eloquent live performers, showcasing at venues as divergent as Japanese concert halls, the biggest American folk festivals and clubs from New York's Bottom Line to Nashville's Bluebird Cafe.

Thirty years down the road, Janis Ian is still greeting each season, each album, each song, each performance with undimmed vitality.

"Actually," says Janis Ian with a chuckle, "I think one of the reasons musicians keep doing what they do and writers keep doing what they do, is that we are totally unsuited for anything else. We really are."

In these pages are the songs of Janis Ian. They are a varied lot. You will find flavors of pop, folk, country, rock, gospel and jazz in them. What unites them all is quality. For each has a melody that tingles the soul and each has a lyric that affects the mind.

This is craftsmanship. This is talent. This is class. This is integrity. This is Janis Ian.

— Robert K. Oermann
Nashville, Tennessee, 1997

ALL ROADS TO THE RIVER

Words and Music by
JANIS IAN and JON VEZNER

Gtr. 1 ⑥ = D

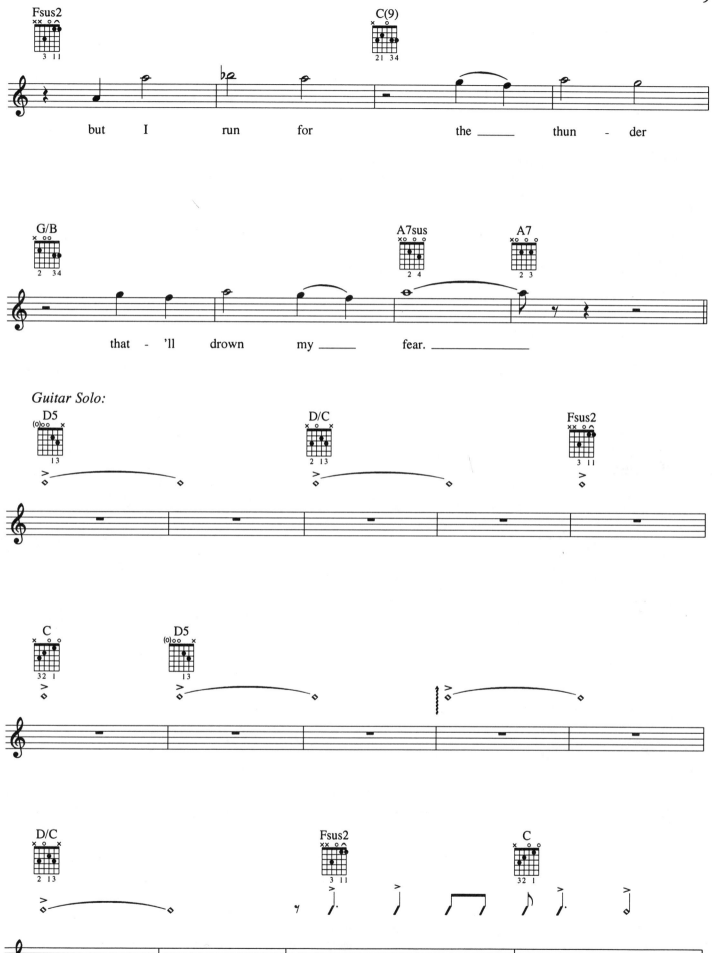

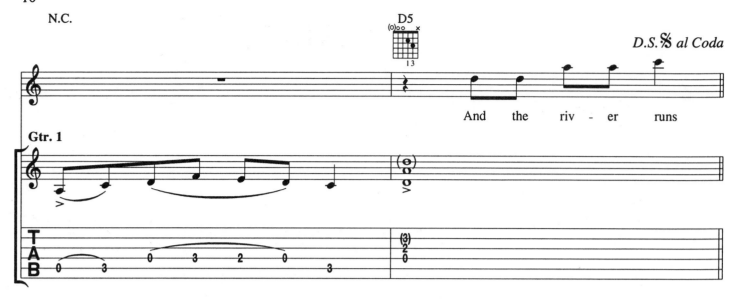

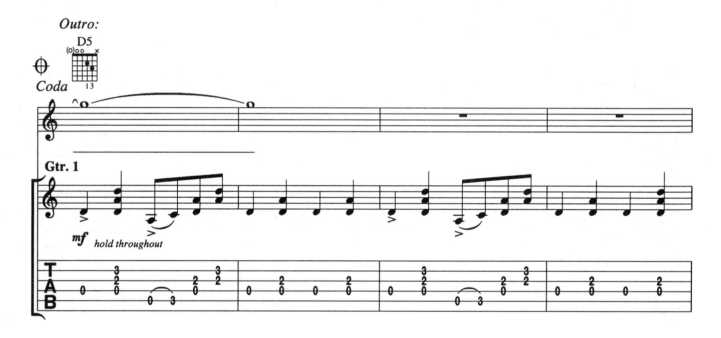

Verse 2:
I am whispering dreams,
I am howling revolutions
All roads to the river.
I am valentine sweet,
I am every mother's nightmare
All roads to the river.

AMSTERDAM

Words and Music by
JANIS IAN and BUDDY MONDLOCK

Amsterdam – 3 – 1
0096B

as I watched __ from the door ___ Just the weight __ of a heart __ as it's fall - ing, noth - ing more _____

Chorus:

I re - mem - ber your lips, __ I re - mem - ber your eyes ___

D.S. %% al Coda

And the taste _ of your kiss, __ and your grace - ful good - bye. You lied. __ Good - bye. __

Coda

freely

___ Good - bye, _____ good - bye, ___ good - bye, __

good - bye.

Bkgd. vcl: Bye.

AT SEVENTEEN

Words and Music by
JANIS IAN

Chorus:

18

Instrumental Solos:
w/Rhy. Fig. 1 *(Gtr. 1) 1st 8 bars*

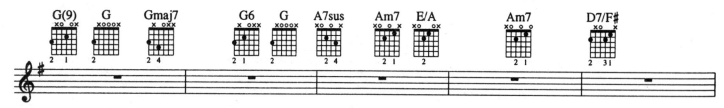

w/Rhy. Fig. 2 *(Gtr. 1) simile*

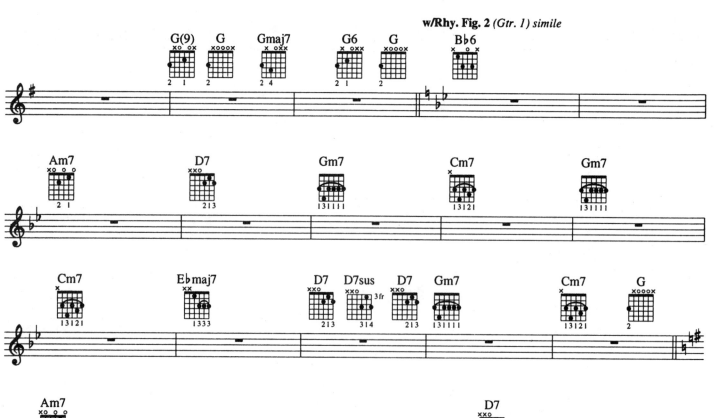

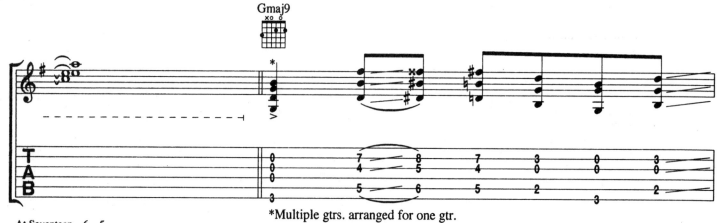

*Multiple gtrs. arranged for one gtr.

Verse 2:
A brown-eyed girl in hand-me-downs
Whose name I never could pronounce
Said, "Pity, please, the ones who serve
They only get what they deserve."
The rich-relationed hometown queen
Marries into what she needs
With a guarantee of company
And haven for the elderly.

Chorus 2:
Remember, those who win the game
Lose the love they sought to gain
In debentures of quality
And dubious integrity
Their small-town eyes will gape at you
In dull surprise, when payment due
Exceeds accounts received, at seventeen.

Verse 3:
To those of us who knew the pain
Of valentines that never came
And those whose names were never called
When choosing sides for basketball
It was long ago and far away
The world was younger than today.
And dreams were all they gave for free
To ugly duckling girls like me.

Chorus 3:
We all play the game, and when we dare
We cheat ourselves at solitaire
Inventing lovers on the phone
Repenting other lives unknown
That call and say, "Come dance with me"
And murmur vague obscenities
At ugly girls like me, at seventeen.

DAYS LIKE THESE

Words and Music by
JANIS IAN

Verse 2:
It's years like these that make a young man old
Bend his back against the promises that life should hold
They can make him wise, they can drive him to his knees
Nothin' comes for free in days like these.

Verse 3:
In lives like these, when ev'ry moment counts,
I add up all the things that I can live without.
When one thing left is the placing of my dreams,
Then I can make my peace with days like these.
I can make my peace with days like these.

EMMANUEL

Words & Music by
JANIS IAN and KYE FLEMING

Gtr. 1 ⑥ = D

Moderately ♩ = 88

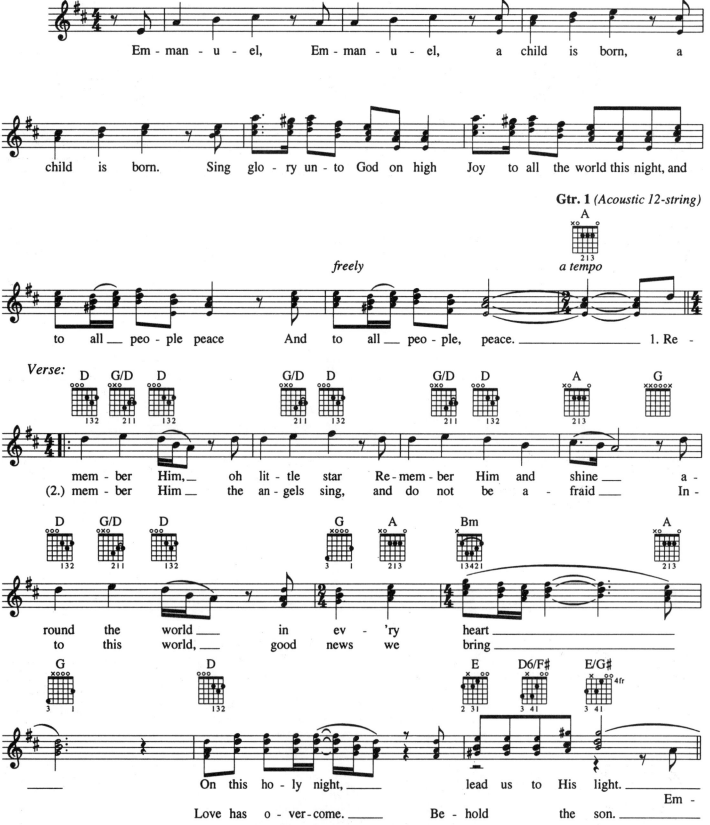

Chorus:

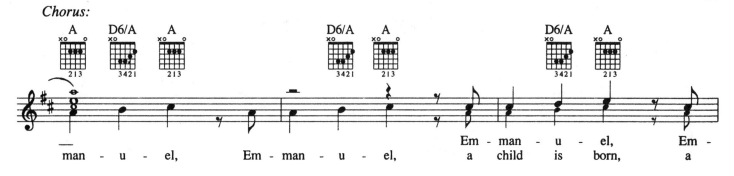

man - u - el, Em - man - u - el, Em - man - u - el, a child is born, a

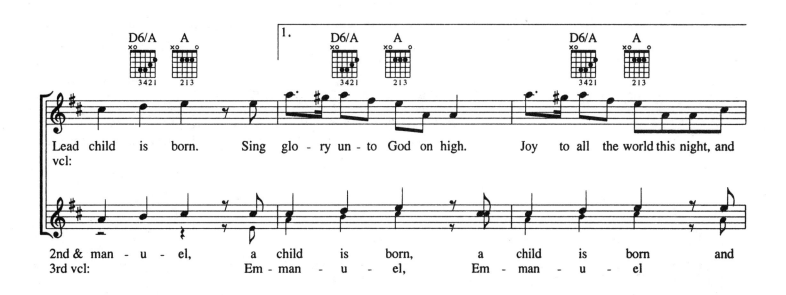

Lead child is born. Sing glo - ry un - to God on high. Joy to all the world this night, and
vcl:

2nd & manuel, a child is born, a child is born and
3rd vcl: Em - man - u - el, Em - man - u - el

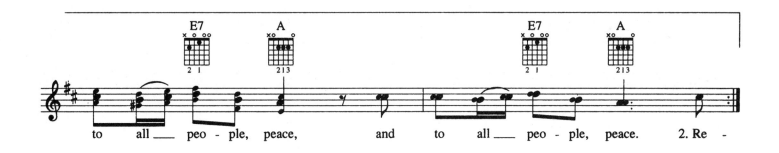

to all ___ peo - ple, peace, and to all ___ peo - ple, peace. 2. Re -

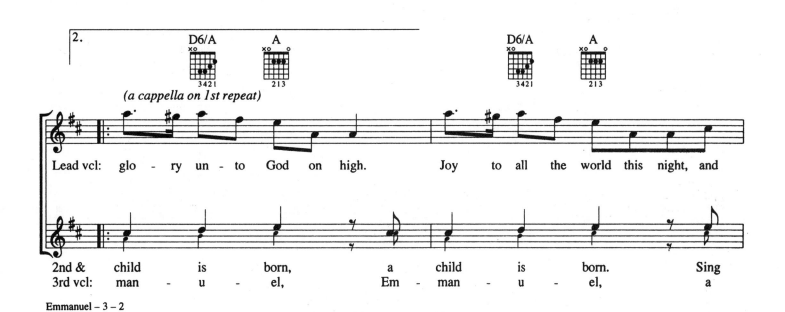

(a cappella on 1st repeat)

Lead vcl: glo - ry un - to God on high. Joy to all the world this night, and

2nd & child is born, a child is born. Sing
3rd vcl: manuel, Em - man - u - el, a

Emmanuel – 3 – 2
0096B

24

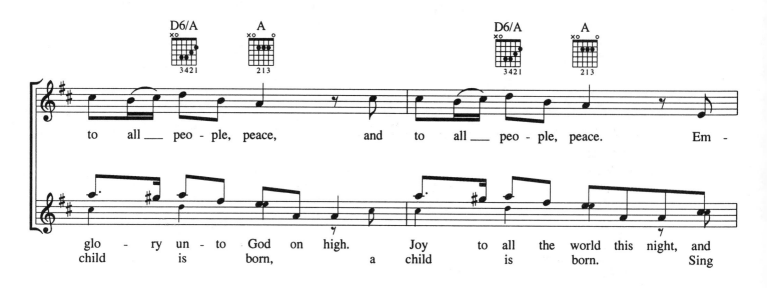

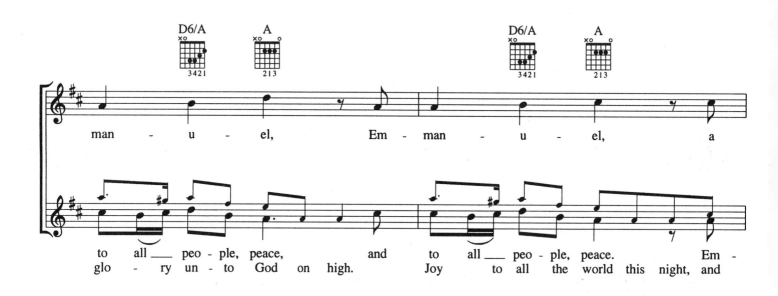

Play 3 times and fade

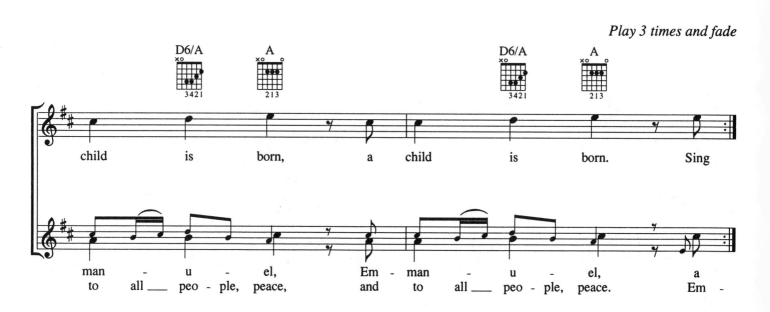

FLY TOO HIGH

Words and Music by
JANIS IAN and GIORGIO MORODER

Gtr. 1 capo I

Moderately fast dance beat ♩ = 128

Intro:

*Gtr. 1

*Keybd. arranged for gtr. w/ flanger effect.
**w/muted trumpet on repeat.

1. A -

Verse:

non - y - mous, au - ton - o - mous will like - ly get the best of us yet ___
2.3. *See additional lyrics*

Be - fore you dis - ap - pear if you can lend me half an ear I'll re - gret ___

___ If I treat ___ you like a num - ber, it's be -

Fly too High – 5 – 1
0096B

Horn Interlude:
N.C.

*Gtr. 1

mf

*Horns arranged for gtr.; vocal tacet on repeat.

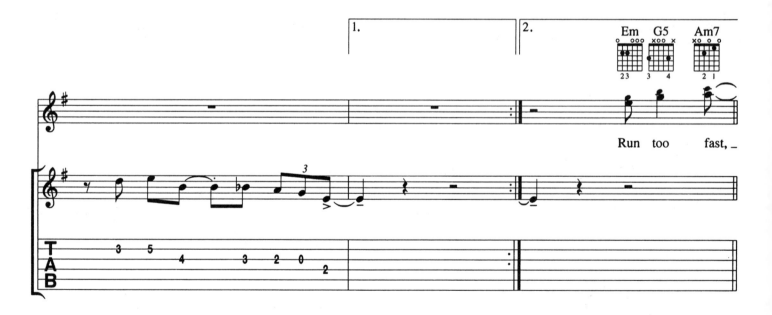

1.

2.

Em G5 Am7

Run too fast, ___

Chorus:

C7   Em7   Am7

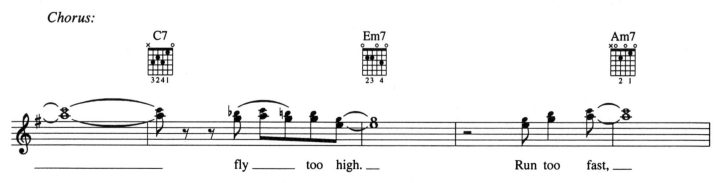

_____ fly ___ too high. ___   Run too fast, ___

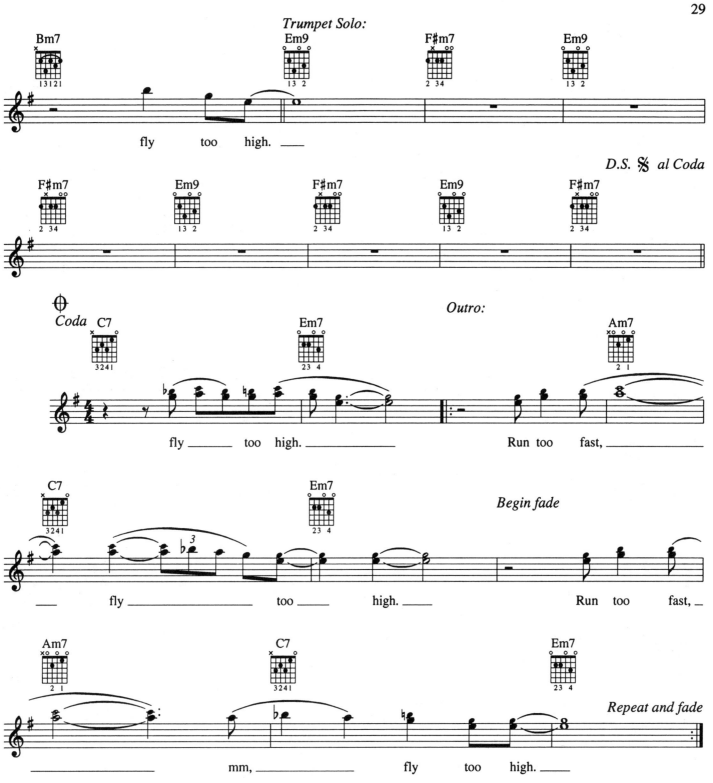

Verse 2:
On dark and lonely nights,
I'm only right
When things are bright on the floor
Dancing and romancing,
Gallivanting with a handsome I score
And if you don't believe me
You should see me
When I'm ready to roar
'Cause I lose my concentration
With a new infatuation, I'm sure
(To Chorus:)

Verse 3:
Hanging around on the infield,
What do you steal
But another feel at the top
Making believe in the long run,
When a shotgun
Is the way to get out of the shop
Hang tail in a new jail
You can go bail
You can dance until you drop
'Cause there's no fool
Like an old fool
In a new school
You just can't stop
(To Chorus:)

FROM ME TO YOU

Words and Music by
JANIS IAN

Gtr. 1 capo I
⑥ = D

Moderately ♩ = 94
Intro:

*Two or more gtrs. arranged here as one gtr. To match record key, capo I.

From Me to You – 7 – 1
0096B

Verse 3:

peo - ple who sur - round __ you, on - ly want __ to see __ you weak __ e - nough __ to crawl __

__ They'll lie for you, __ de - cide __ for you, __ and buy __

__ up all __ your rights __ and all __ your wrongs __ And they'll

try to stop your sing - ing in the mid - dle of your song For they

do not want you free __ and they will not make you strong, __ but on - ly drag __

__ you down __ in the hole they're com - ing from __ 4. They

34

Verse 4:

say   you   are   fool - ish   in   want - ing   the   sun _____

Say   you   are   sel - fish _____   in   learn - ing   to   run __

Tell   you   that __   the   dark - ness   is   a   bless-ing   in   dis - guise, _   for   you

nev - er   have _   to   no - tice _____   if   you're   sight - ed   or ___   you're   blind _   And   they'll

do   their   best   to   keep _   you   from _   the   light _____

5. You're

Verse 5:

more than be-gin-ning, you're learn-ing to fly. ___ You

feel like you're fall-ing, ___ but it pass-es in time ___ And I

hate to see ___ a friend ___ go down ___ in flames ___ with-out a song ___ So I'm

wait-ing by the door-way, but I will not lin-ger long ___ And I'm

D.S. 𝄋 al Coda

36

Coda

GETTING OVER YOU

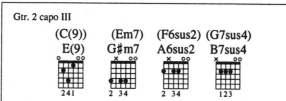

Words and Music by
JANIS IAN and GARY BURR

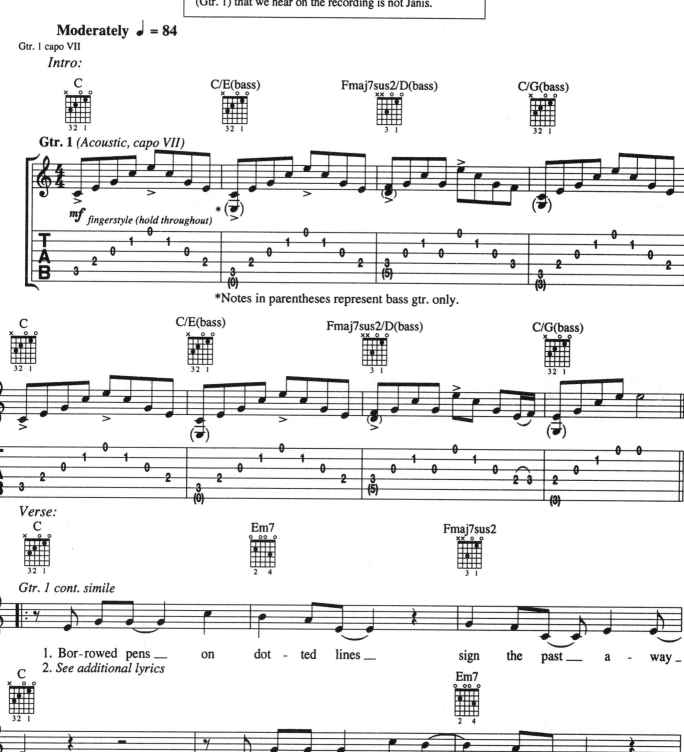

Getting Over You – 3 – 1
0096B

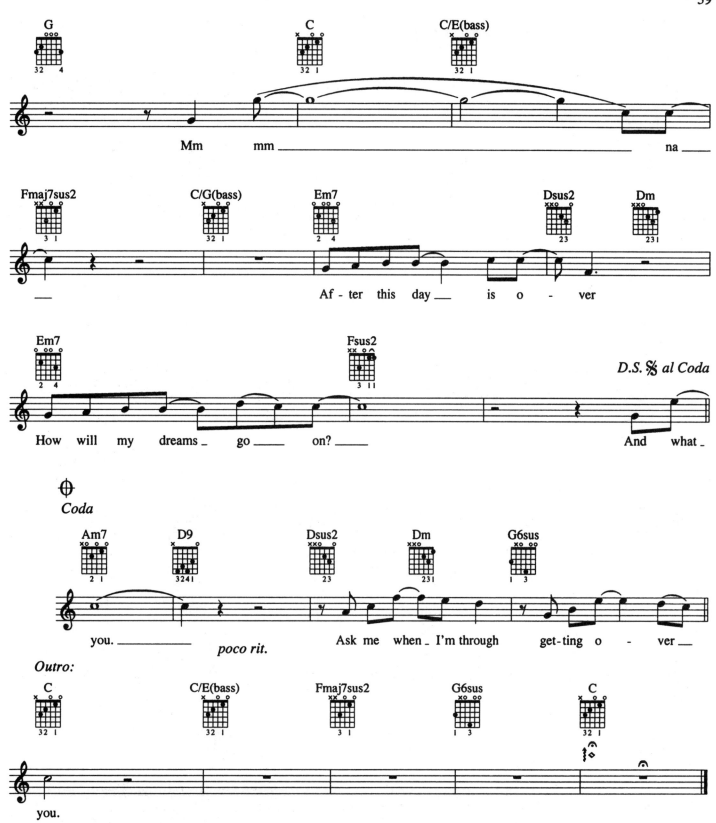

Verse 2:
Tell me what you see in her
That used to be in me
Why is it the simple truths
Are hardest to believe
How can I start all over
Knowing we'll just be friends?
(To Pre-Chorus:)

HONOR THEM ALL

Words and Music by
JANIS IAN

To match record, capo II

Gtr. 1 capo II ⑥ = D

Moderately fast ♩ = 110

Intro:

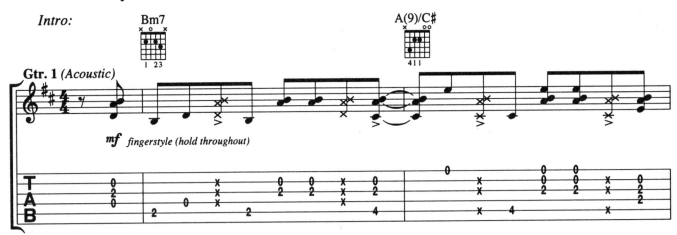

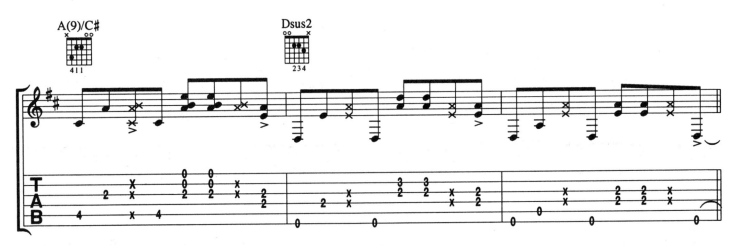

Honor Them All – 5 – 1
0096B

Play bracketed chords on repeat only.

42

Each time you rise ___ or you fall _____ Hon - or them ___ all

Bridge:

have three neph-ews, all ___ my chil - dren, and my mem - o - ries ___

___ If there's one thing I ___ would ask, ___ it's that they

keep a - live ___ the past ___ so the fu - ture does - n't have ___

___ to end ___ with ___ me ___ I want them to hon -

Chorus:

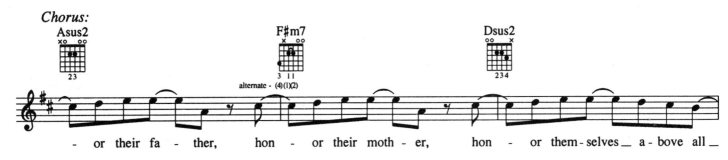

- or their fa - ther, hon - or their moth - er, hon - or them - selves __ a - bove all __

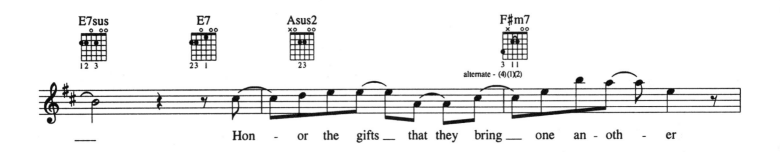

__ Hon - or the gifts __ that they bring __ one an - oth - er

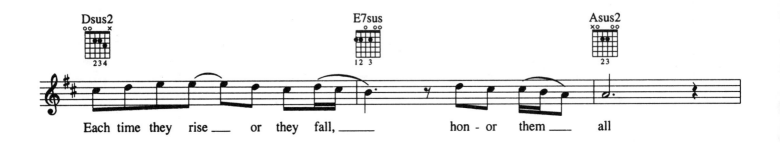

Each time they rise __ or they fall, _____ hon - or them __ all

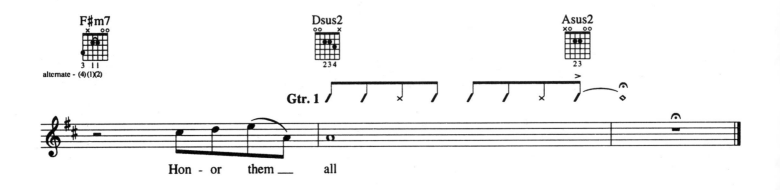

Hon - or them __ all

Verse 2:
There's not a family on this earth
Doesn't sling a little mud
Hands get weary, hearts get hurt
We bow to the flesh and blood

Pre-Chorus:
Oh, people can be cruel sometimes
And it leaves a lasting scar
But when you put it to the test
You usually find they've done their best
And, as bad as that may be
It's turned you into who you are, so why don't you...
(To Chorus:)

JESSE

Words and Music by
JANIS IAN

Moderately slow ♩ = 86

Intro:

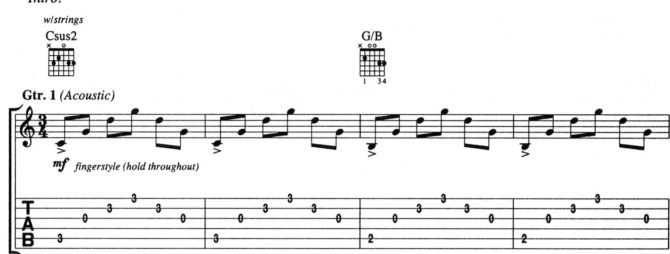

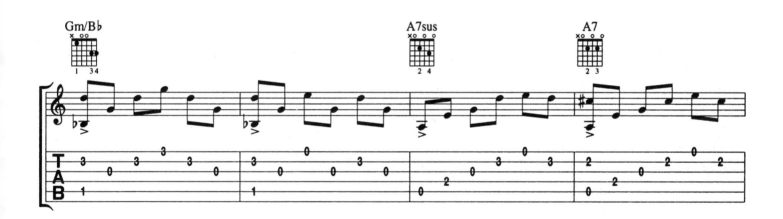

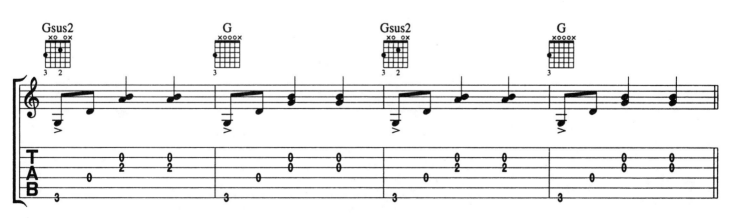

Jesse – 5 – 1
0096B

46

48

D.S. 𝄋 al Coda

Verse 2:
Jesse, the floors and the boards,
Recalling your steps,
And I remember too.
All the pictures are fading,
And shaded in grey,
But I still set a place
On the table at noon.
(To Chorus:)

Verse 3:
Jesse, the spread on the bed
Is like when you left
I've kept it up for you.
All the blues and the greens
Have been recently cleaned,
And it's seemingly new.
Hey, Jes me and you

Chorus 3:
We'll swallow the light on the stairs
We'll do up my hair and sleep unaware.
Hey, Jesse, I'm lonely
Come home.

LOVE IS BLIND

All gtrs. capo III

Words and Music by
JANIS IAN

Moderately slow in 2 ♩ = 70

Intro:

*Capo 3 to match record key.

Verse:

blind   love is   on - ly sor - row _____   love is

2.3. *See additional lyrics*

no to-mor - row   since you ___ went a - way   Love is

To Coda ⊕

blind,   how well I re-mem - ber _____   In the

Verse 2:
Love is blind
Love is without a mercy
Love is, "Now you've hurt me
Now you've gone away"
Love is blind
Love is no horizon
And I'm slowly dying
Here in yesterday.

Chorus 2:
In the morning
Waken to the sound of weeping
Someone else should weep for me
Now it's over
Lover, let me be.

Verse 3:
Love is blind
Love is your caress
Love is tenderness
And momentary pain
Love is blind
How well I remember
In the heat of summer pleasure
Winter fades.

RIDE ME LIKE A WAVE

Words and Music by
JANIS IAN

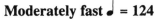

Gtr. 1 capo III

⑥ = D

Moderately fast ♩ = 124

Intro:

Gtr. 1
(Acoustic)

*simile throughout
unless written otherwise*

Verse 1:

1. Hide me in ___ your hol - lows   Taste the salt ___ that clings ___ to me ___

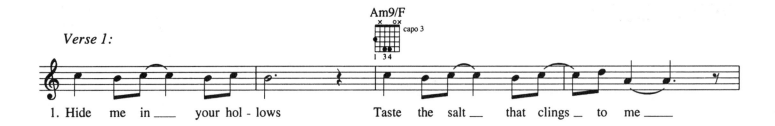

Ship-wrecked in your ___ shal - lows, ___   scent - ed by ___ the sea ___

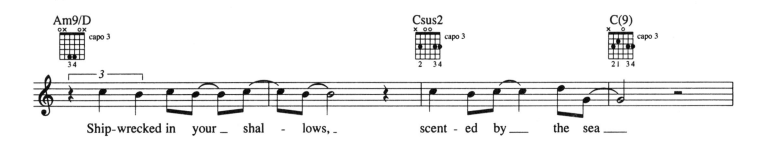

Hide me in ___ the wis - dom of ___ your thighs ___   Ride me like ___

Ride Me Like a Wave – 4 – 1
0096B

RUBY

Words and Music by
JANIS IAN and KYE FLEMING

looks fade ___ too fast ___ Ru - by's got a past ___ But when she's

Chorus:

sleep - ing ___ a - lone, she dreams of cleans - ing ___ her ___ soul

Just like they prom - ised ___ in ___ church But the

Sun - days seem ___ to come and go like the preach-ers on ___ the ra - di - o ___

1.

poco rit.

2.

Verse 3:

3. Some sell their bod - ies for dimes

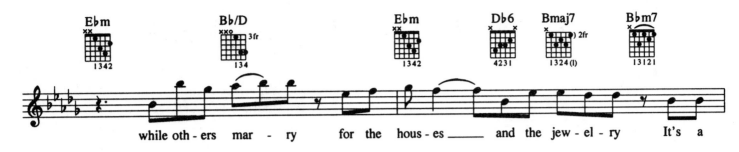

while oth-ers mar-ry   for the hous-es _____ and the jew-el-ry   It's a

real _____ thin   line _____   what you __ charge for your time. _____

Outro:

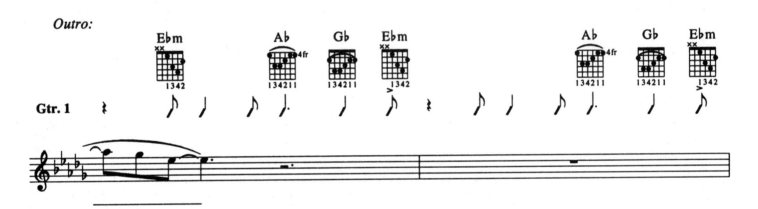

Gtr. 1

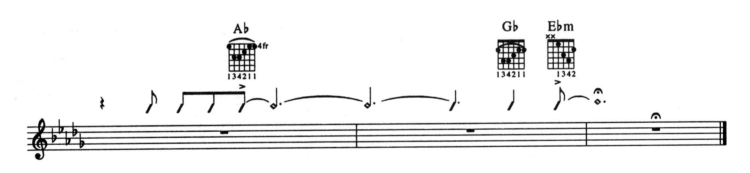

Verse 2:
Above the noise and the neon
There's a saxophone
Playing smoky old familiar notes
That float up the stairs
Ruby takes a rose from her hair
Sees her face in the mirror
Wipes her cheek with a tear
Under the makeup, she longs to be touched
Ruby don't ask for much.
(To Chorus:)

SEARCHING FOR AMERICA

Words and Music by
JANIS IAN

Searching for America – 5 – 1
0096B

Dsus2

1. Where

Verse:

Csus2   G/B   Dsus2

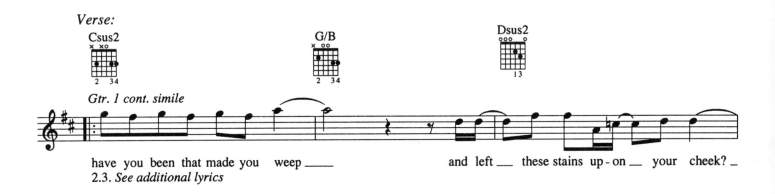

Gtr. 1 cont. simile

have you been that made you weep _____ and left __ these stains up-on __ your cheek? _

2.3. *See additional lyrics*

Csus2   G/B

What did you see while you were gone _____ that haunts _

Dsus2   Asus2

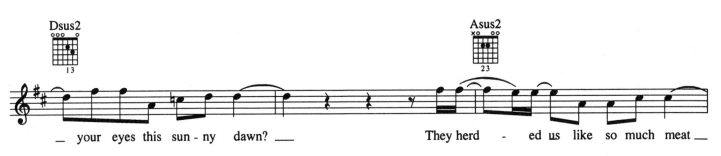

__ your eyes this sun-ny dawn? __ They herd - ed us like so much meat __

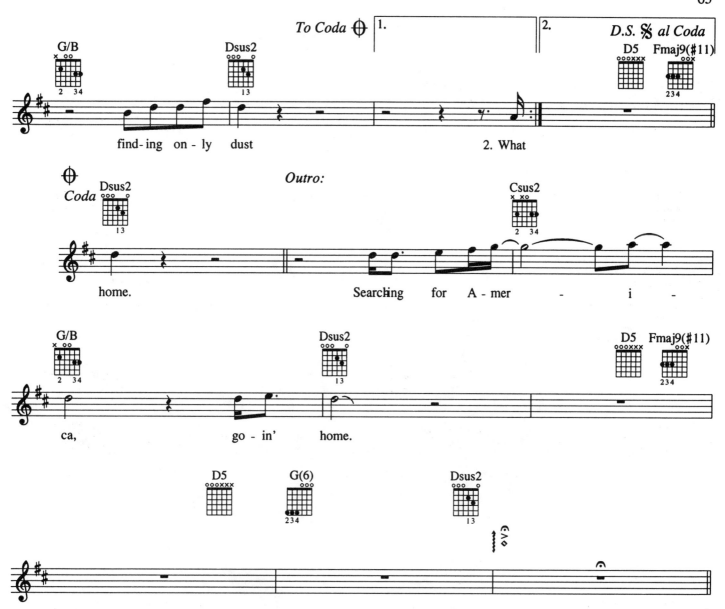

Verse 2:
What did you see that made you cry
And left these trackmarks on your eye?
What did you find while you were there
That sucks the light out of the morning air
They gave us each a cropper's shack
And land so hard it broke the back
Then fed us 'til our bellies burst
On promises that died at birth
So I lay the baby out each dawn
In between the tender corn
With sunrise for her bonnet
And flies her only blanket
We harvested until we bled
'Til every single root ran red
And when the work was finally done
They gave our names to immigration
I did not know how bad it hurt
Until I lay there eating dirt
And the cold seeped in between my bones
That's where I was when I left home

Chorus:
Searching for America
All her dreams and hopes
Searching for America
Finding only ghosts

Verse 3:
Who are these people you have seen
To dream this dark and distant dream?
To tell the stories you have told
To leave these bruises on your soul
They are the flesh, they are the bone
They are the very cornerstone
They leave their mansions and their shacks
To hide here in between the cracks
Their hope is tattooed on my lips
Bleeding from my fingertips
They are crawling toward the promised land
Hand over hand
To walk until they run no more
And wash up on some distant shore
Where truth is not the enemy
And whatever does not kill us, sets us free
Somewhere out there
Are millions just like me
Homesick for Eden
Heartsick at the memory

Chorus:
Searching for America
In every stick and stone
Searching for America
Going home
Seaching for America
Going home

"Society's Child"

With Leonard Bernstein during the taping of "Inside The Pop Revolution." I was 15 at the time and "Society's Child" had been banned nationwide for a year. Bernstein featured me and the song for an astonishing 15 minutes. The next morning, radio stations began apologizing and playing it.

*With Chick Corea after recording my song "Jenny" for the **Night Rains** album.*

Philadelphia Folk Festival, 1971 with David Bromberg

Philadelphia Folk Festival, 1973 with Steve Goodman.

With Mel Torme.

Steve Earle, Connie Bradley, Johnny Cash, Janis Ian and Clint Black

At a Nashville function with Clint Black and Mary Chapin Carpenter. I worked with Chapin's long-time co-producer John Jennings on my Revenge album.

Performing "When Angels Cry" on "General Hospital."

*With Joan Baez, Paradiso, Amsterdam
May 3, 1993*

*With Ani Di Franco cutting
"Searching for America."*

© 1993 Jim Forest

Photo: Patricia Snyder

On tour with Mary Black.

*With Chet Atkins. Chet's first words to me when we
met were "Play me something great!" as he handed
me his guitar. He's recorded a number of my songs—
I love working with him.*

*With Kathy Mattea and Deana Carter
recording "Emmanuel"*

*With Melissa Etheridge—she interviewed me for a cover story in
The Advocate and cited me as a major influence.*

SOCIETY'S CHILD
(a/k/a "Society's Child (Baby I've Been Thinking)")

Words and Music by
JANIS IAN

All gtrs. capo III

Moderately fast ♩ = 106

Intro:

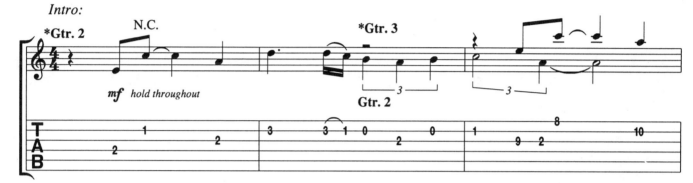

*Harpsichord arranged for two gtrs.

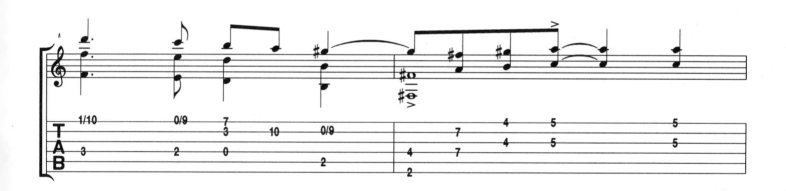

Society's Child – 3 – 1
0096B

Verse:
accel. a tempo (on repeats)

a tempo ♩ = 106

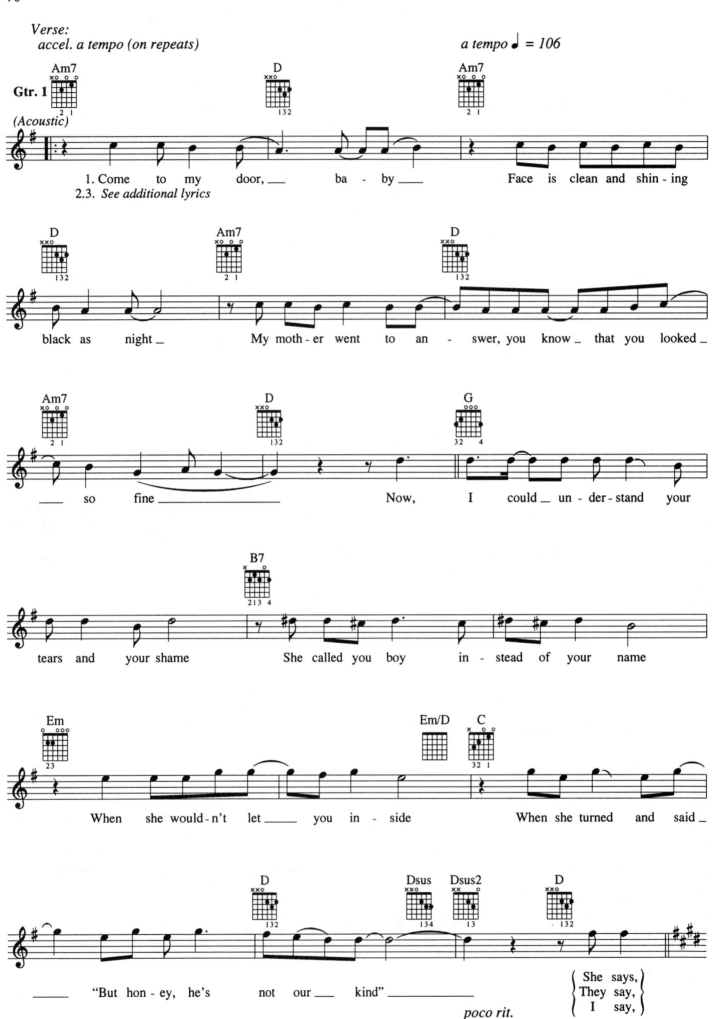

1. Come to my door, ___ ba - by ___ Face is clean and shin - ing
2.3. *See additional lyrics*

black as night ___ My moth - er went to an - swer, you know ___ that you looked ___

___ so fine _____ Now, I could ___ un - der - stand your

tears and your shame She called you boy in - stead of your name

When she would - n't let ___ you in - side When she turned and said ___

_____ "But hon - ey, he's not our ___ kind" _____ She says, They say, I say,

poco rit.

Slower ♩ = 94

Chorus:

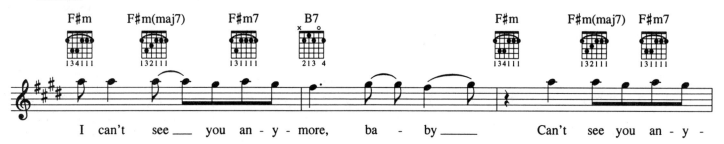

I can't see — you an-y-more, ba — by ——— Can't see you an-y-

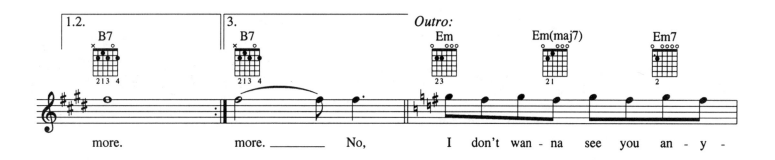

more.   more. ——— No,   I don't wan-na   see   you   an-y-

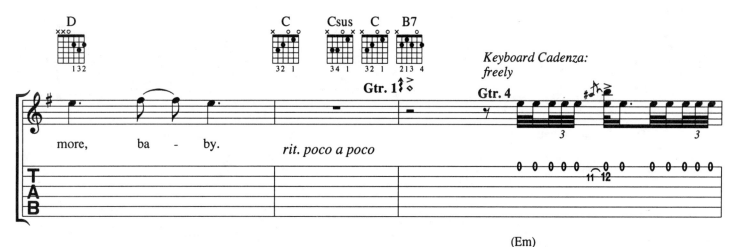

more,   ba — by.   *rit. poco a poco*

Keyboard Cadenza:
freely

Gtr. 1   Gtr. 4

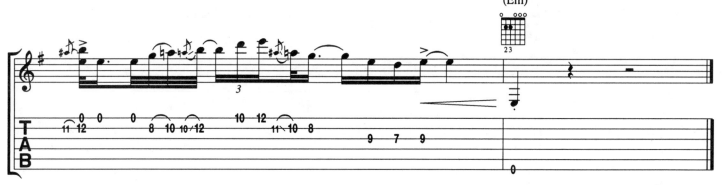

Verse 2:
Walk me down to school, baby
Everybody's acting deaf and blind
Until they turn and say
"Why don't you stick to your own kind?"
My teachers all laugh, their smirking stares
Cutting deep down in our affairs
Preachers of equality
Think they believe it
Then why won't they just let us be?
(To Chorus:)

Verse 3:
One of these days I'm gonna stop my listening
Gonna raise my head up high
One of these days I'm gonna
Raise up my glistening wings and fly.
But that day will have to wait for a while,
Baby, I'm only society's child
When we're older, things may change
But for now this is the way they must remain.
(To Chorus:)

SILLY HABITS

Words and Music by
JANIS IAN

Slow jazz ♩. = 64

Intro: 𝄋 *Verses :*

1. I'm _ still in love, though I don't care _ to let you know _____
2.4. *See additional lyrics*
3. *Piano Solo on D.S.*
* Guitar strums '4 to the bar.'

There's some-thing there _ It does-n't show _____ But when you're near,

To Coda ⊕

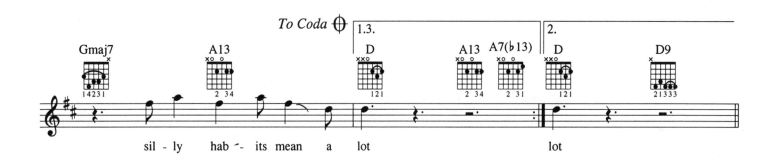

sil - ly hab - its mean a lot   lot

Bridge:

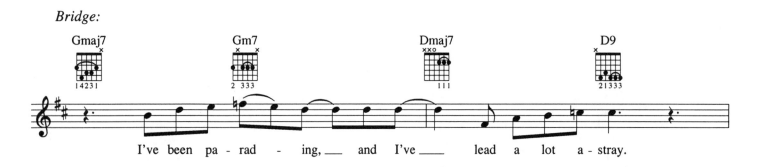

I've been pa - rad - ing, ___ and I've ___ lead a lot a - stray.

Silly Habits – 2 – 1
0096B

Why __ both-er wait - ing when you can have it all __ to - day? _____

___ You may re - mem - ber ___ I like my cof - fee hot _____

D.S. 𝄋 al Coda
(with repeat)

Sil - ly hab - its mean a lot

Coda

Outro:

Gtr. 1

lot.

Verse 2:
I've been alone now
For quite some time, it's true
But every night when I come home
I'm coming home to you
I listen for your footsteps
Sometimes I even knock
Silly habits mean a lot

Verse 4:
So you go your way
And I'll go mine
Maybe one day our paths will re-entwine
I used to say "I love you"
But one day I forgot
Silly habits mean a lot

STARS

Gtr.1 capo I

Words and Music by
JANIS IAN

Moderately slow ♩ = 78

Intro:

Gtr. 1 *(Acoustic)*

mf *fingerstyle (hold throughout)*

I was nev-er one for sing-ing   what I _____ real-ly feel _____

ex-cept to-night   I'm bring-ing   ev-'ry-

Stars – 10 – 1
0096B

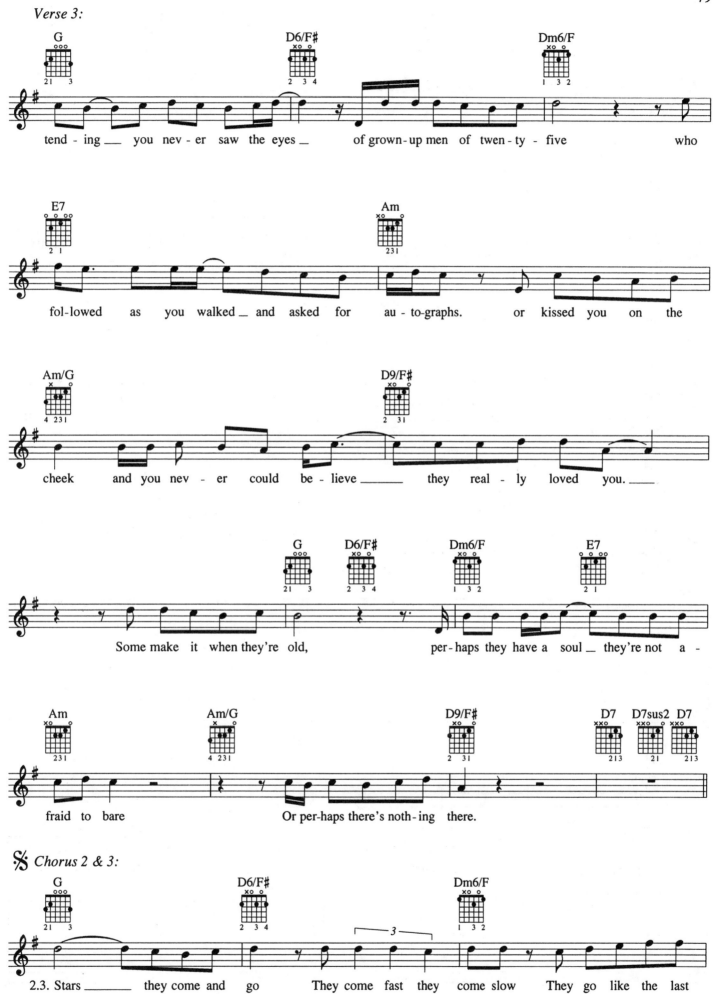

Verse 3:

tend - ing ___ you nev - er saw the eyes ___ of grown - up men of twen - ty - five who

fol - lowed as you walked ___ and asked for au - to-graphs. or kissed you on the

cheek and you nev - er could be - lieve _____ they real - ly loved you. ___

Some make it when they're old, per - haps they have a soul ___ they're not a -

fraid to bare Or per-haps there's noth - ing there.

Chorus 2 & 3:

2.3. Stars _____ they come and go They come fast they come slow They go like the last

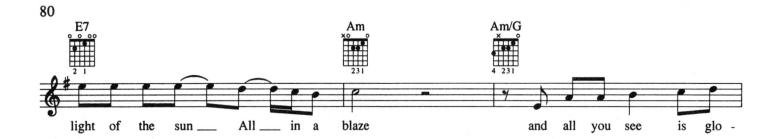

light of the sun ___ All ___ in a blaze and all you see is glo-

ry

But most ___ have seen it all, they
(3.) But those ___ who've seen it all live

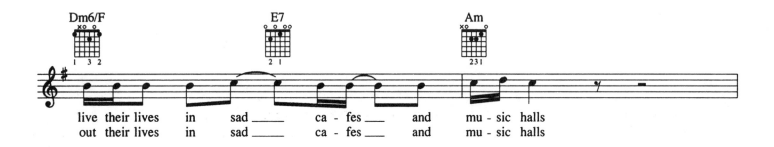

live their lives in sad _____ ca-fes ___ and mu-sic halls
out their lives in sad _____ ca-fes ___ and mu-sic halls

To Coda

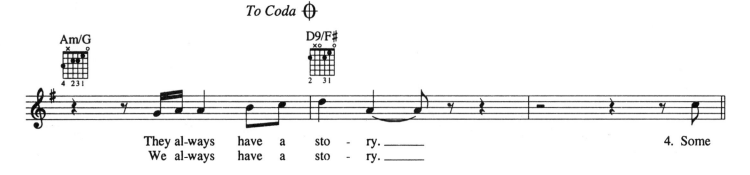

They al-ways have a sto-ry. _____
We al-ways have a sto-ry. _____ 4. Some

Verse 4:

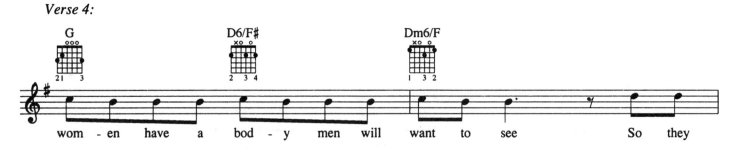

wom-en have a bod-y men will want to see So they

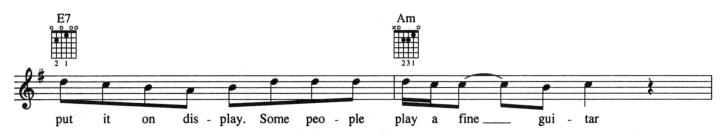

put it on dis-play. Some peo-ple play a fine ___ gui-tar

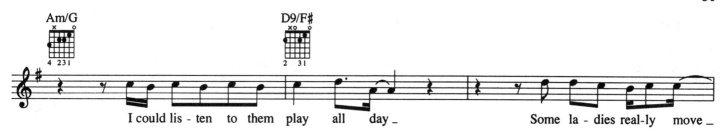

I could lis - ten to them play all day _ Some la - dies real - ly move _

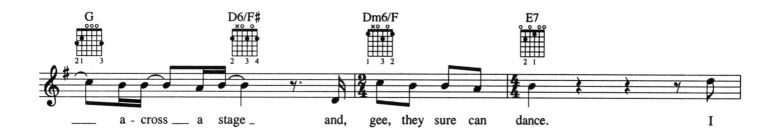

_____ a - cross ___ a stage _ and, gee, they sure can dance. I

guess I could learn how if I gave it half _ a chance. _ But I

al - ways feel so fun - ny ___ when my bod - y tries to soar. And I

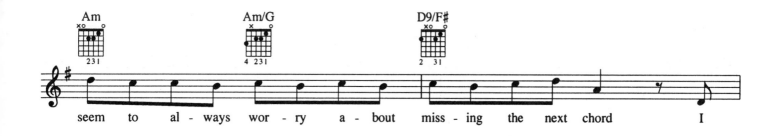

seem to al - ways wor - ry a - bout miss - ing the next chord I

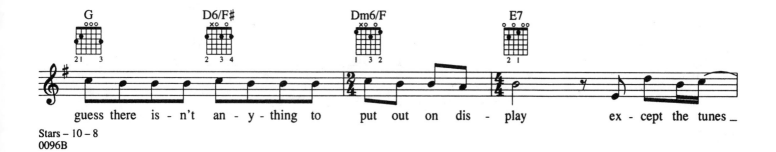

guess there is - n't an - y - thing to put out on dis - play ex - cept the tunes _

Stars – 10 – 8
0096B

and what-ev-er else I say   2. And an-y-

Bridge 2:

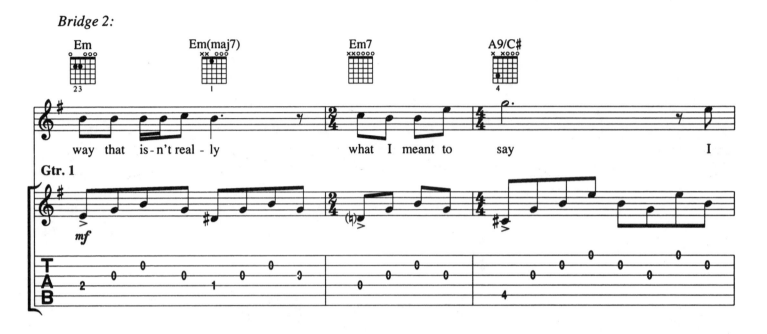

way that is-n't real-ly   what I meant to say   I

Gtr. 1

Freely

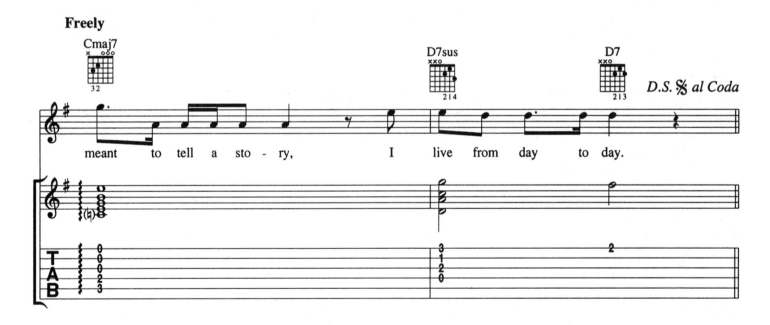

meant to tell a sto-ry,   I live from day to day.

D.S. 𝄋 al Coda

Coda

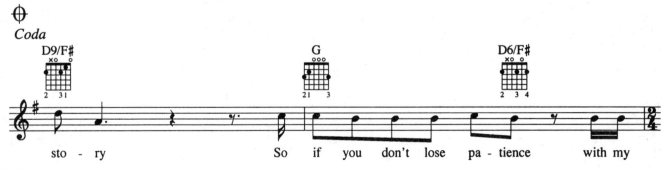

sto-ry   So if you don't lose pa-tience   with my

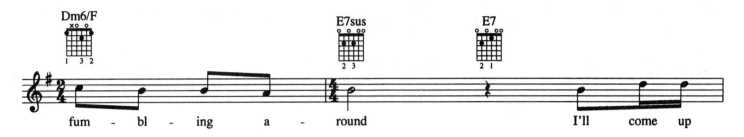

fum - bl - ing a - round   I'll   come   up

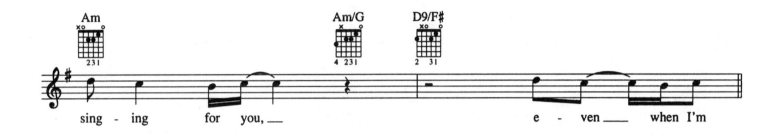

sing - ing for you, ___   e - ven ___ when I'm

Outro:

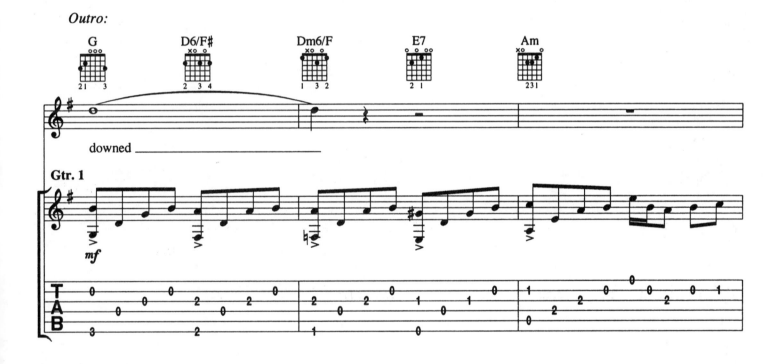

downed _____

Gtr. 1

mf

hold _____

SOME PEOPLE'S LIVES

Words and Music by
JANIS IAN and KYE FLEMING

Some People's Lives – 3 – 1
0096B

and

and they never know why

Chorus:

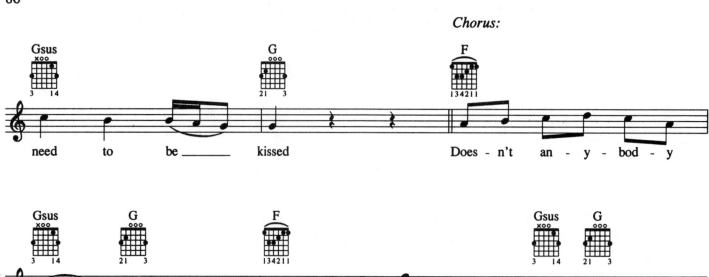

need to be _____ kissed   Does-n't an-y-bod-y

tell _____ them?   Does-n't an-y-bod-y see?

Freely

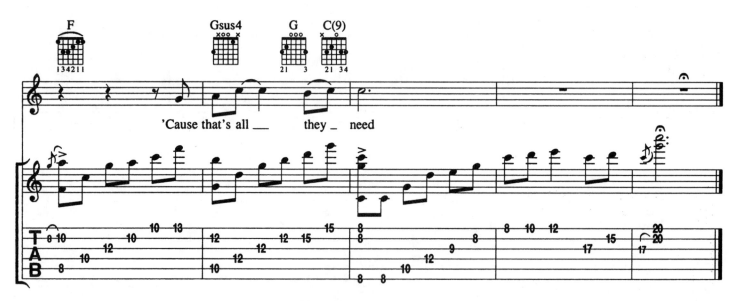

Does-n't an-y-bod-y love them ___   like you ___ love me?

'Cause that's all ___ they _ need

Verse 2:
Some people's eyes
Fade like their dreams.
Too tired to rise,
Too tired to sleep.
Some people laugh
When they need to cry,
And they never know why.

TAKE NO PRISONERS

Words and Music by
JANIS IAN

Gtr. 1 capo II
⑥– D

Moderately fast ♩ = 114

Intro:

Verse:

Dm7 ... **Dm6**

1. The writ-er wrote   The sing-er sung
2. *See additional lyrics*

The rec-ord broke   The au-di-ence _ was stunned

Some they begged for mer-cy __   Oth-ers e-ven cried _____

A7sus ... **Dm7**   N.C.

Some they fled, left for dead, _ some said it changed _ their _ lives

1. And the
2. *See additional lyrics*

Gtr. 1

Pre-Chorus:

Gm7 ... **Am7**

writ-er said "I wish _ you'd known me __   when
3. lov-er said "Why don't _ you touch me? __

Bb6 ... **Csus2**

I still __ be-lieved in __ the truth   Now it's
Reach out __ your hand just __ like this   You can

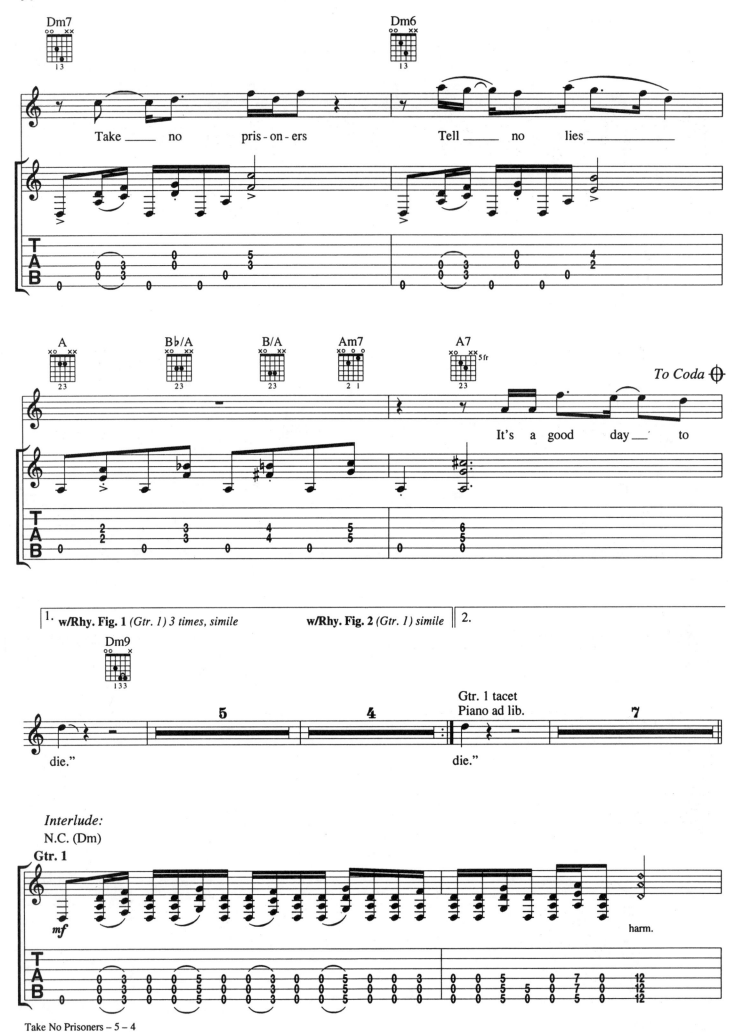

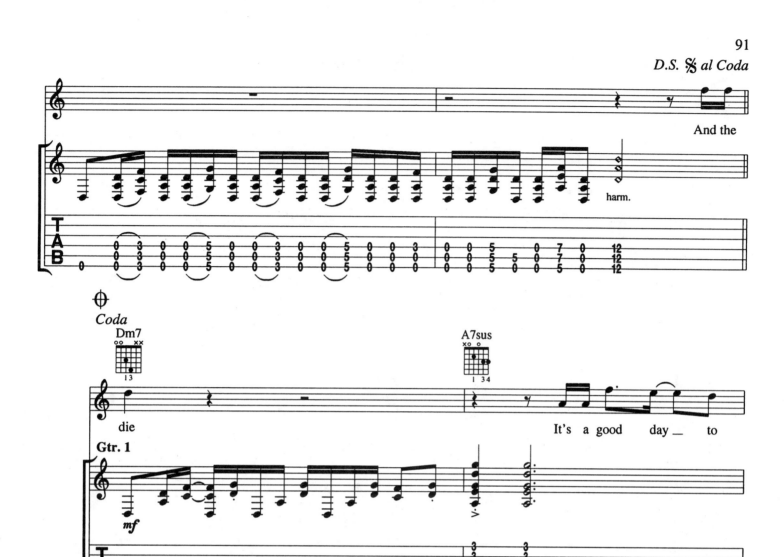

Verse 2:
God spoke
The people laughed
The tablets broke
While they were pissing on the golden calf.
Some they found their heaven
Others found their hell
Some they ran to Canaan Land
Some just lay where they fell.

Pre-Chorus 2:
And God said "Hey I wish you'd known me
When I still believed you'd be true
Now for the rest of your days
When you call out my name
I'll be Mister God to you."
(To Chorus:)

TATTOO

Words and Music by
JANIS IAN

Gtr. 1 capo I
⑥= D

Moderately ♩ = 94

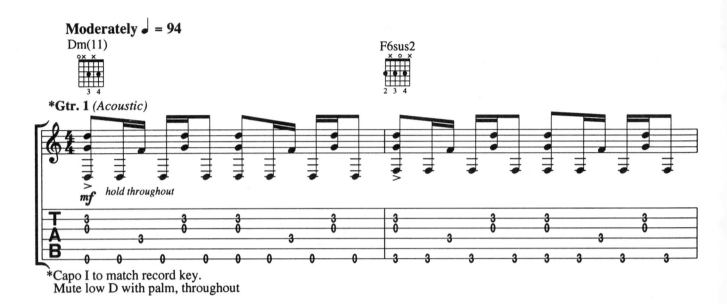

*Capo I to match record key.
Mute low D with palm, throughout

1. Her new name ___ was tat-tooed to her wrist ___
2.3. See additional lyrics

Tattoo – 7 – 1
0096B

It was long - er than the old _____ one _____

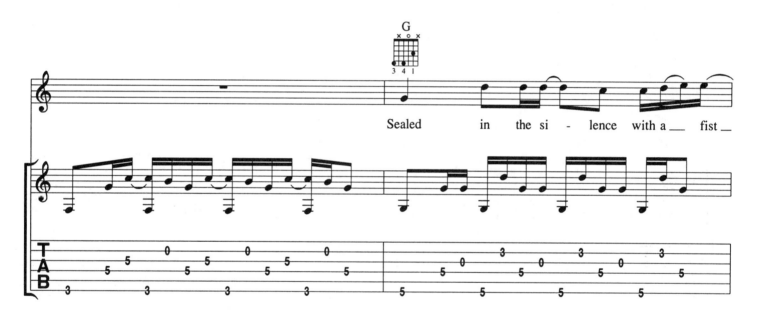

Sealed   in the si - lence with a ___ fist __

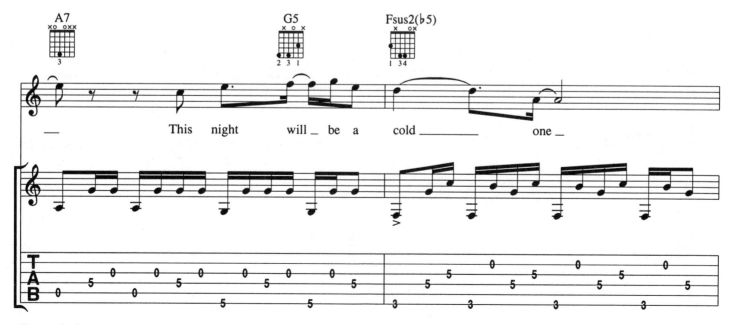

This   night   will __ be a   cold _____ one __

Tattoo – 7 – 2
0096B

Tattoo – 7 – 4
0096B

Verse 2:
She steps out of line to the left,
And her father to the right
One side's a cold, clean death
The other is an endless night
Gold from a grandmother's tooth
Mountains of jewelry and toys
Piled in the corners
Mailed across the borders
Presents for the girls and boys
Presents for the girls and boys
Tattoo

Verse 3:
Soldiers from the other side
Liberated them at dawn
Gave her water, gave her life
She still had all her clothes on
She lived until she died
Empty as the autumn leaves that fly
Surgeons took the mark
But they could not take it far
It was written on her heart
Written on her empty heart
Tattooed

THE OTHER SIDE OF THE SUN

Words and Music by
ALBERT HAMMOND and JANIS IAN

The Other Side of the Sun – 3 – 1
0096B

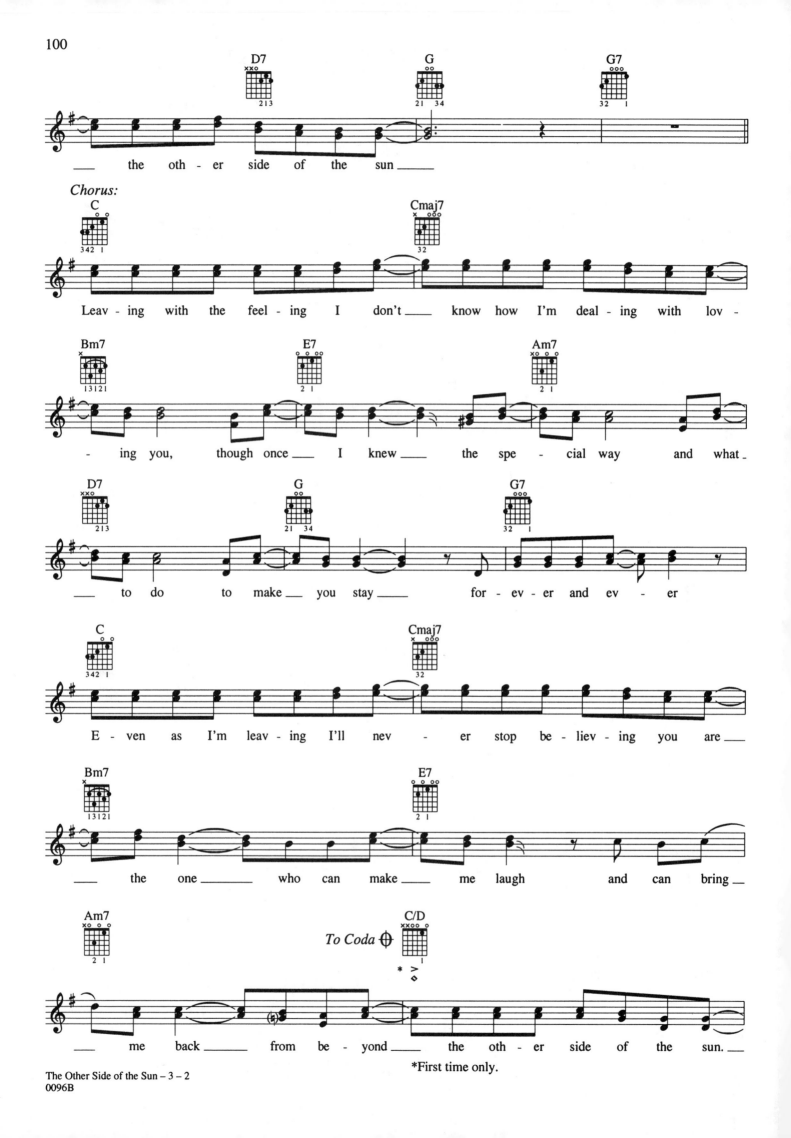

*Played by Bass gtr.

Outro:

Verse 2:
Rolling down the river
I hope I can deliver the morning
Wishing on a star
For the sun to come out and play
Funny when it's over
You really don't remember the warning
You might as well be living
Out beyond the Milky Way
(To Chorus:)

THIS OLD TOWN

Gtr. 1 capo II

Words and Music by
JANIS IAN and JON VEZNER

Moderately in 2 ♩ = 88

Intro:

1. This old town should-'ve burned down in nine-teen twen-ty-nine ___
2. *See additional lyrics*

That's when we stood in ___ line ___ Wait-ing for ___ our soup, ___ while

swal-low-ing ___ our pride ___ This old town should-'ve burned down in

nine-teen thir-ty-one, ___ when the rain re-fused ___ to come ___

This Old Town – 4 – 1
0096B

Coda

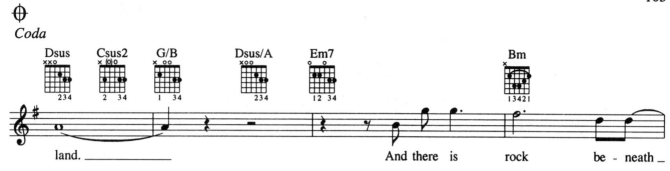

land. _____ And there is rock be - neath _

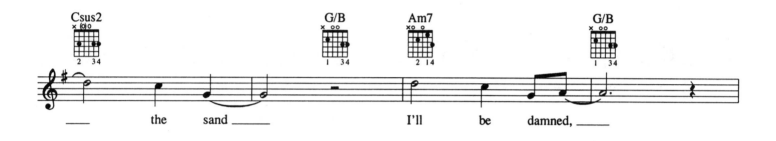

____ the sand _____ I'll be damned, _____

Outro:
w/Rhy. Fig. 1 *(Gtr. 1)*
1st 3 measures, simile

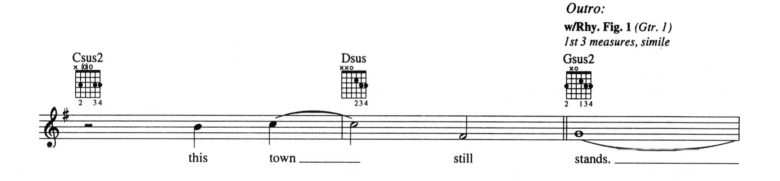

this town _____ still stands. _____

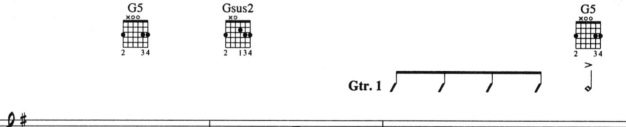

Gtr. 1

____

Verse 2:
This old town should've burned down in 1944
When the last man went to war
They came back different, if they came back at all
This old town should've burned down in 1956
That's when the twister hit
And all our hopes lay buried beneath the boards and bricks
And we almost called it quits
(To Chorus:)

THIS TRAIN STILL RUNS

Words and Music by
JANIS IAN and JESS LEARY

Guitar capo II,
strings 6, 5, 4, 3, tuned:

⑥- D   ③- G

⑤- A   ②- B

④- D   ①- E

This song uses an interesting tuning. Janis uses a Kyser capo across the 6th, 5th, 4th and 3rd strings at the 2nd fret with the 6th stringed tuned to D. In the tab and chord diagrams, the four capoed strings are indicated as 0 with the tab numbered from there. For the two strings not capoed, "0" indicates the nut. (To match recording, tune down a 1/2 step.) Or you can tune your guitar: D A D G A D. Either way, the tab and chord diagrams work.

Verse:

1. I felt a rum-ble in __ my heart, __
(2.) __

o - ver the moun-
back _____ at the sta -

This Train Still Runs – 4 – 1
0096B

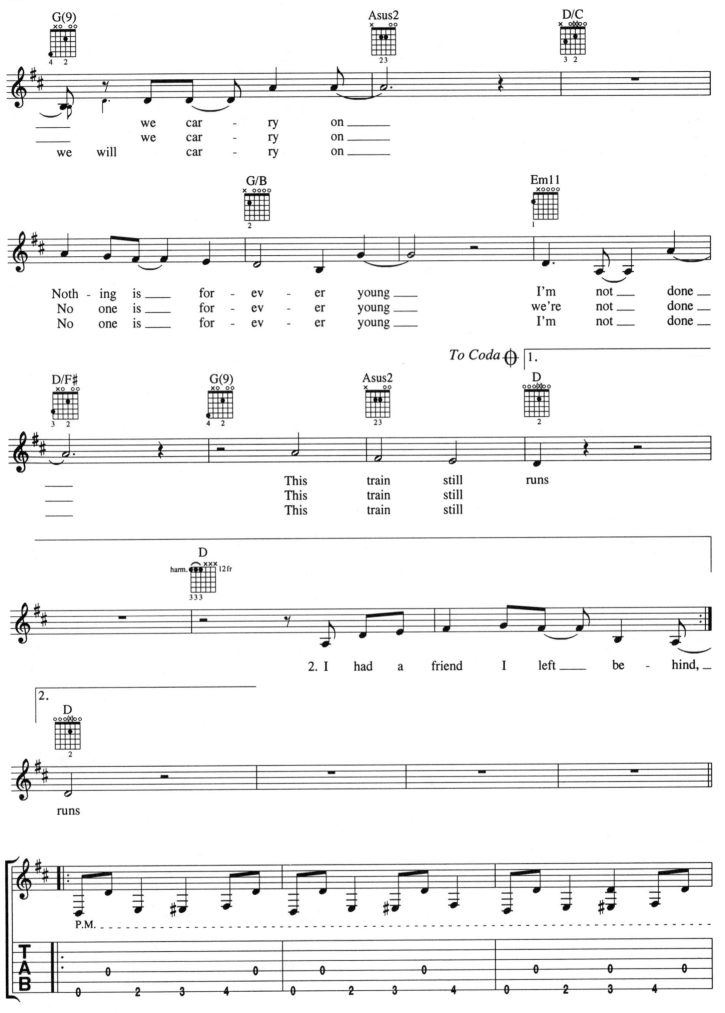

WELCOME TO ACOUSTICVILLE

Words and Music by
JANIS IAN

Gtr. 1 capo III
⑥ = D

*Basic tonality.

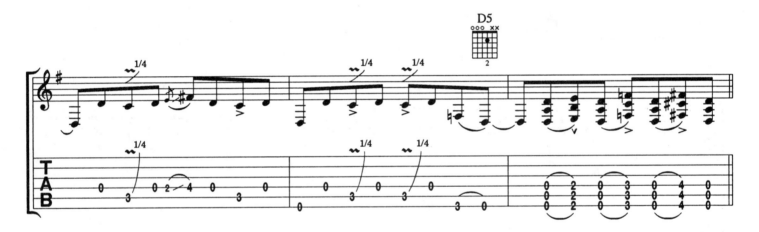

  Verse:

1. It was a long, ___ long ___ road ___ It was a big ___ deep ___ hole, ___
2. 3. *See additional lyrics*

Welcome to Acousticville – 12 – 1
0096B

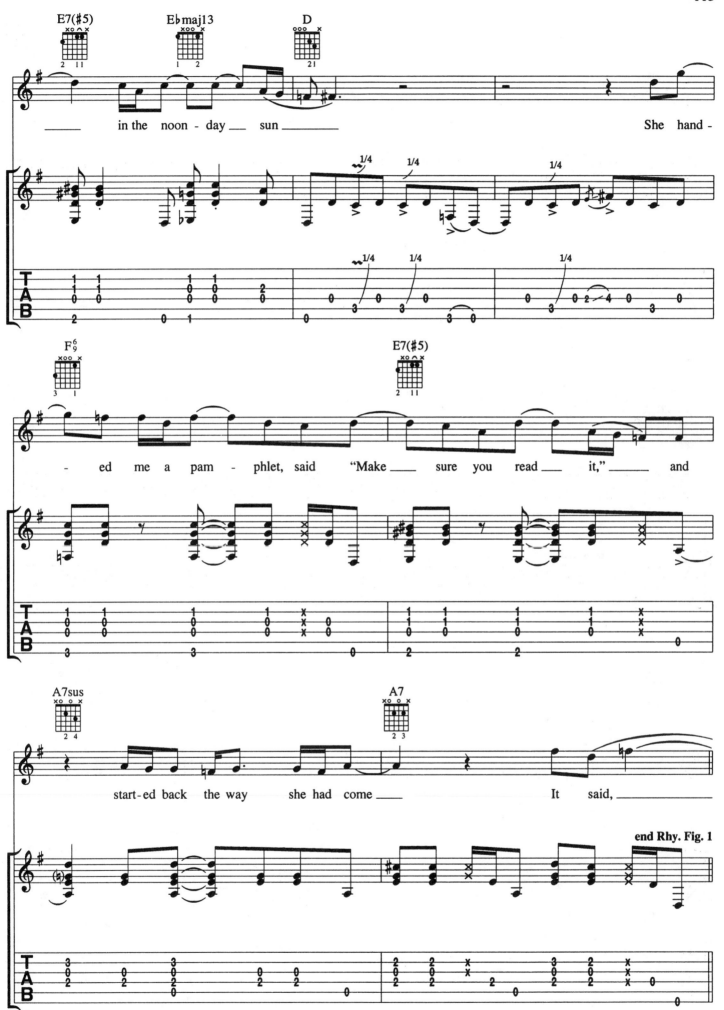

Hen - drix played a big old D-eight-een _____ and we all _____ joined in as he _____ be - gan _ to scream, "Wel - come to A - cous - tic - ville." _____

end Rhy. Fig. 2

Guitar Solo:

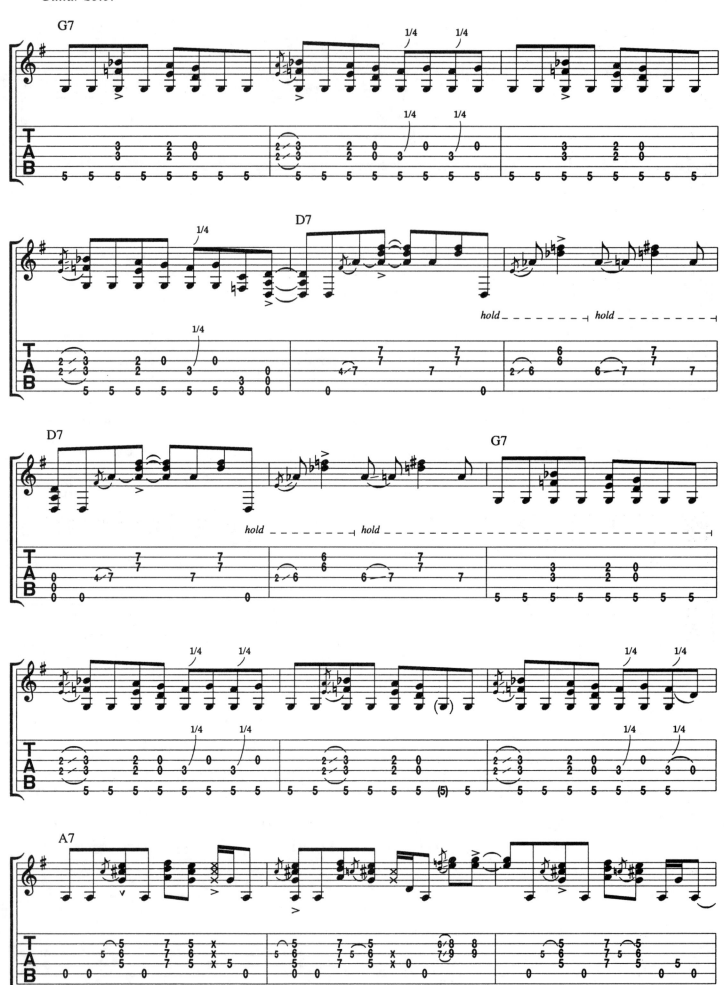

w/Rhy. Fig. 2 *(Gtr. 1) simile*

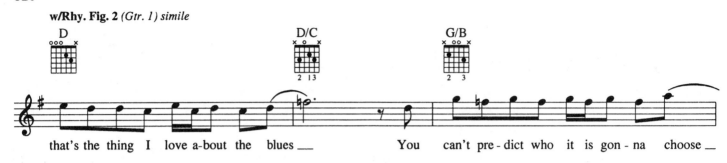

that's the thing I love a-bout the blues ___ You can't pre-dict who it is gon-na choose ___

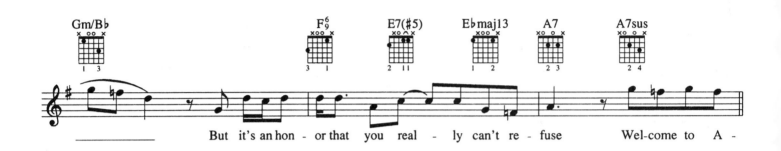

___ But it's an hon - or that you real - ly can't re - fuse Wel-come to A -

Outro:

cous - tic - ville ___ Wel - come to A - cous -

Gtr. 1

tic - ville ___ Wel - come to A - cous -

Verse 2:
It was a big mirage
Or maybe her garage
Just looked like a Motel Six
She checked me in right there
Wearing nothing but her hair
And a couple of candlesticks
She had long, long teeth
It was a huge relief
That the door had a chain
It was and ordinary bed
It had a sign that said,
"You can steal this stain"

Pre-Chorus 2:
Not an outlet in sight
Not a lamp, not a light
And it was coming on night
I was sleeping on the floor
When she slithered through the door
And whispered, "Baby did you lose your appetite?"

Chorus 2:
She said, "Welcome to Acousticville
Welcome to the place where time stands still
Ain't no bass, ain't no drums
Ain't no waste, just two opposable thumbs
Welcome to Acousticville"

Verse 3:
It was a real good time
Good food, good wine
I got my appetite back
But whenever I told her I wanted to leave
She'd get so mean
She'd peel the paint off a Cadillac
"Wait a minute," I said
"I don't recall being dead
Though I am white as a ghost"
She looked me right in the eye
Said, "You think you're alive but baby,
God only knows"

Coda:
And that's the thing I love about the blues
You can't predict who it is gonna choose
But it's an honor that you really can't refuse
Welcome to Acousticville
Welcome to Acousticville
Welcome to Acousticville

WHEN ANGELS CRY

Words and Music by
JANIS IAN

Gtr. 1 capo II

Slowly ♩ = 62

Verse 1:

1. Wait, your tired ___ arms must rest Let this mo - ment pass. Wait un - til the morn - ing

Close your eyes and let me see who you used to be

Gtr. 1 *(Acoustic)*

mf fingerstyle (hold throughout)

be Left with - out ___ a warn - ing

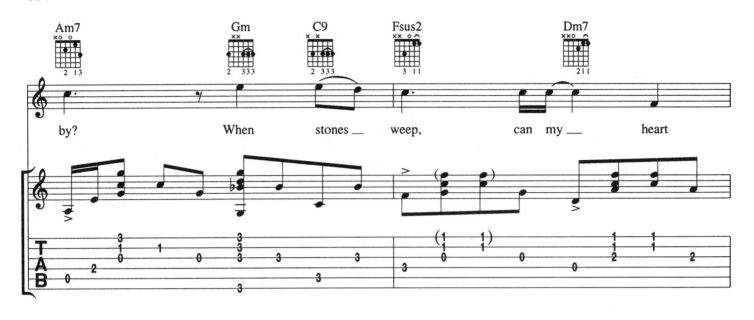

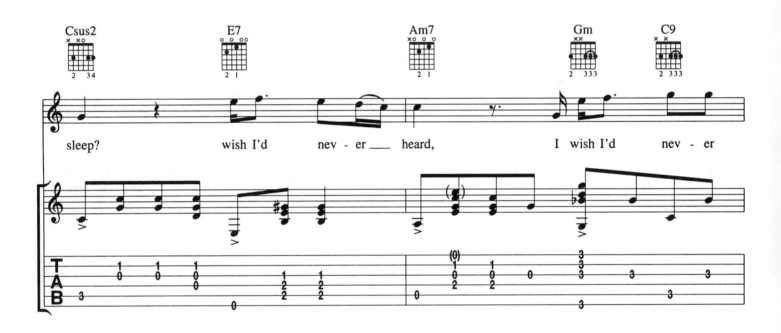

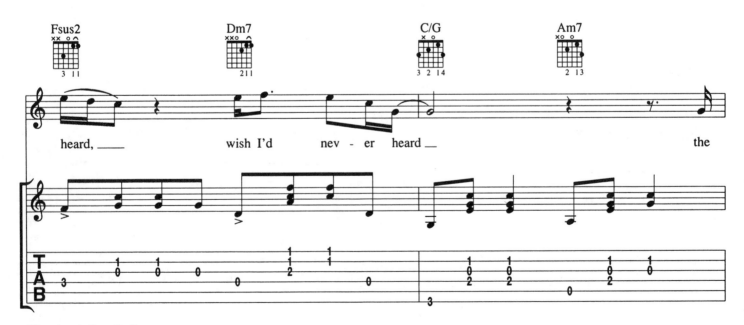

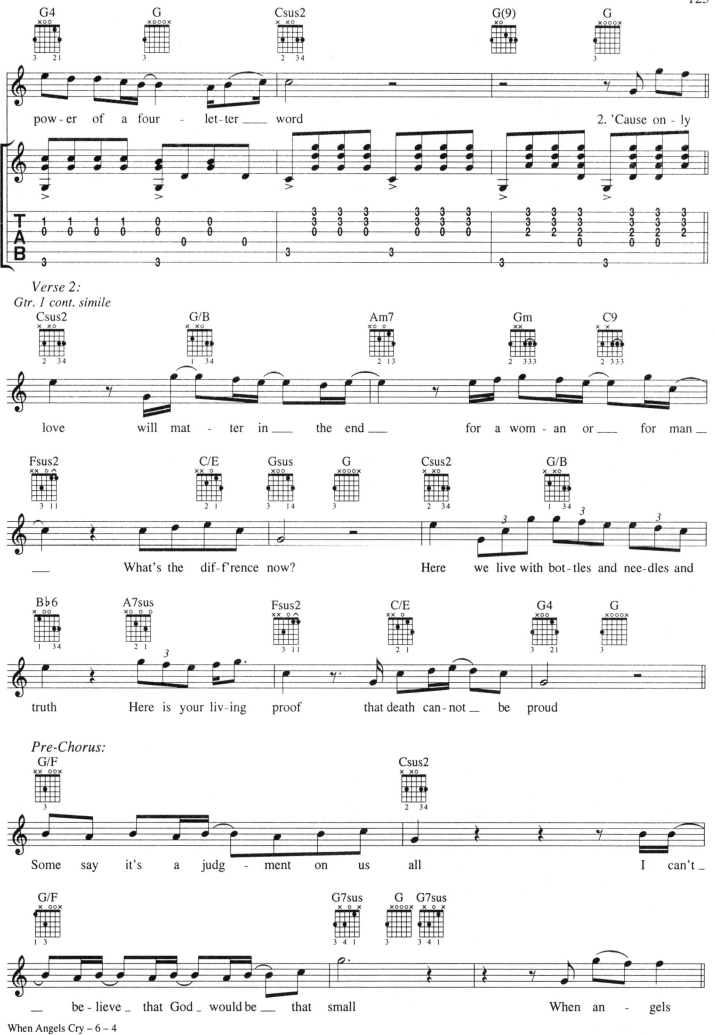

WHAT ABOUT THE LOVE

Words and Music by
JANIS IAN and KYE FLEMING

Verses 1, 2 & 4:

went to see __ my sis - ter   She was stay-ing with _ a friend __ who had
2.4. See additional lyrics

turned in - to __ a preach - er   to save the world _ from sin ___   He said,

What About the Love – 7 – 1
0096B

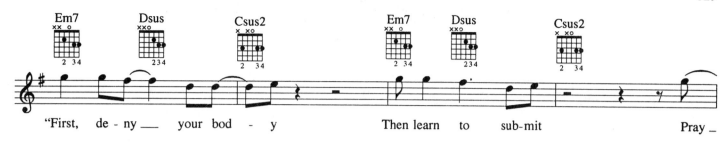

"First, de - ny ___ your bod - y   Then learn to sub-mit   Pray _

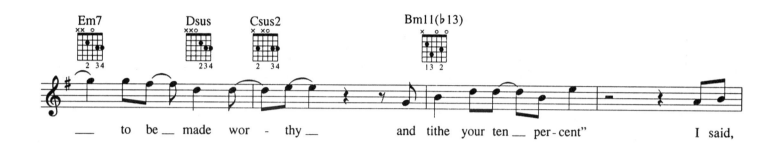

___ to be ___ made wor - thy ___   and tithe your ten ___ per - cent"   I said,

"Is this all ___ there is? ___   Just the let - ter of ___ the law? _

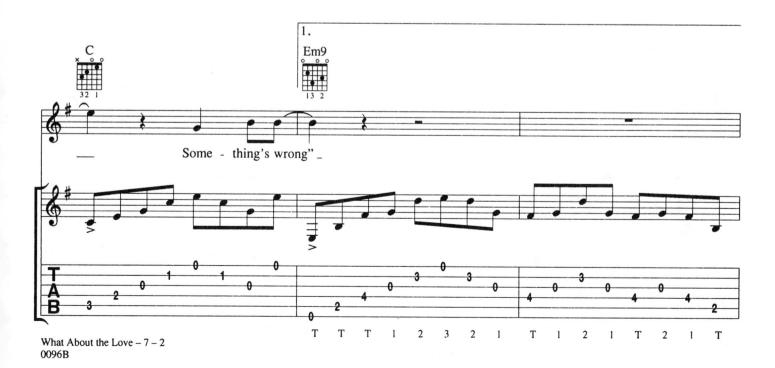

Some - thing's wrong" _

Csus2

B7(#9)

To Coda ⊕

a - bout the love, what __ a - bout the love, what _____ a - bout the love?" ___

Em7 Dsus Csus2 Em7 Dsus Csus2

3. I

Verse 3:

Em7 Dsus Csus2 Em7 Dsus

went to see __ my neigh - bor He'd been tak - en to ___ a home

Csus2 Em7 Dsus Csus2 Bm11(♭13)

for the weak and the __ dis - card - ed who have no place _ to go

Em7 Dsus Csus2 Em7 Dsus

He said, "Here I lack _ for noth - ing I am fed and I ____ am _ clothed _

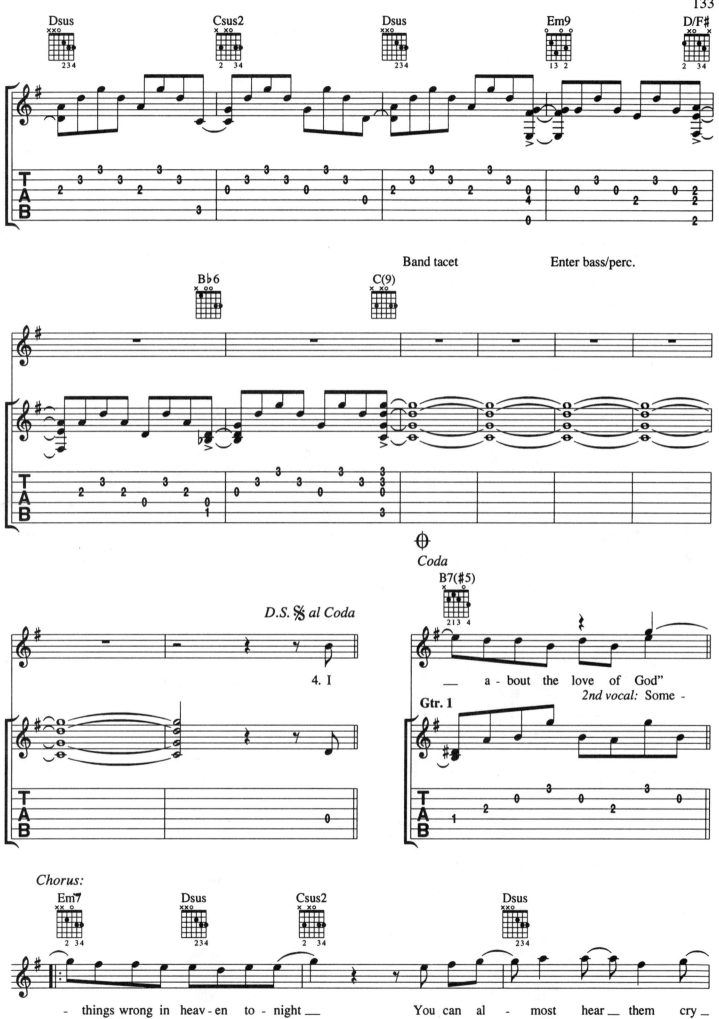

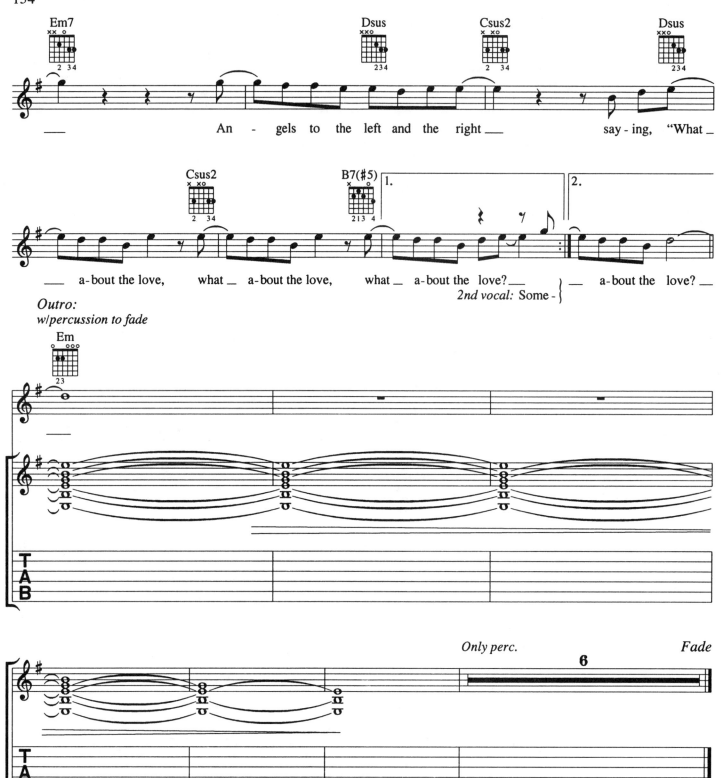

Em7　　　　　　　　　　Dsus　　Csus2　　Dsus

An - gels to the left and the right ___ say - ing, "What _

Csus2　　　　　B7(#5)　　1.　　　　　　　　2.

___ a-bout the love, what _ a-bout the love, what _ a-bout the love?___) _ a-bout the love? ___
2nd vocal: Some - {

Outro:
w/percussion to fade

Em

Only perc.　　　　　6　　　　　Fade

Verse 2:
I went to see my brother
On the thirty-second floor
Of a building down on Wall Street
You could hear the futures roar
He said, "Here we make decisions
And we trade commodities
So if you tell me where there's famine
I can make you guarantees"
I said, "Is this all there is
Power to the strong?
Something's wrong"

Verse 4:
I looked into the mirror
Proud as I could be
And I saw my pointing finger
Pointing back at me
Saying, "Who named you accuser?
Who gave you the scales?"
I hung my head in sorrow
I could almost feel the nails
I said, "This is how it is
To be crucified and judged
Without love"

Janis Ian: DISCOGRAPHY

1966   ***Janis Ian***   Verve/Forecast
      "Society's Child (Baby I've Been Thinking)"
      "Hair of Spun Gold"

1967   ***For All the Seasons of Your Mind***   Verve/Forecast
1968   ***The Secret Life of J. Eddy Fink***   Verve/Forecast
1969   ***Who Really Cares***   Verve/Forecast
1970   ***Present Company***   Capitol
1973   ***Stars***   Columbia
      "Jesse"
      "Stars"

1975   ***Between the Lines***   Columbia
      "At Seventeen"
      "Watercolors"

1976   ***Aftertones***   Columbia
      "Love Is Blind" (a No. 1 hit in Japan for 6 months)
      "Boy I Really Tied One On"

1977   ***Miracle Row***   Columbia
      "I Want to Make You Love Me"

      Betrayal soundtrack   Inner City
      "Betrayal"

1978   ***Janis Ian***   Columbia
      "That Grand Illusion"

1979   ***Night Rains***   Columbia
      "Fly Too High"
      "Here Comes the Night" (theme from ***The Bell Jar***)
      "The Other Side of the Sun" (a hit in Europe)

1980   ***Foxes*** soundtrack   Casablanca
      "Fly Too High"(#1 in Europe, Africa, Australia)

1981   ***Restless Eyes***   Columbia
      "Under the Covers"

      Mel Torme and Friends — Mel Torme   Finesse/CBS
      "Silly Habits" (with Mel Torme)

1982   ***In Harmony 2*** children's album   CBS
      "Ginny the Flying Girl"

1992   ***Falling From Grace*** soundtrack   Mercury
      "Days Like These"

1993   ***Breaking Silence***   Morgan Creek
      "All Roads to the River"
      "Some People's Lives"
      "What About the Love"

1995   ***Revenge***   Beacon
      "Take Me Walking in the Rain"
      "When Angels Cry"

      Ring Them Bells — Joan Baez   Guardian
      "Jesse" (with Joan Baez)

1997   ***Hunger***   Windham Hill
      "Searching for America" (prod. by Ani Difranco)
      "Honor Them All"

      The Carols of Christmas   Windham Hill
      "Emmanuel" (with Deana Carter & Kathy Mattea)

Janis Ian:

CAREER HIGHLIGHTS

The 1960s

1963 — The folk magazine Broadside publishes her song "Hair of Spun Gold;" Janis is 12 years old.

1964 — First paid performance, $36 from a club in New Jersey.

1965 — At age 14 she begins singing in New York folk clubs.

1966 — Signs with Verve/Folkways Records. "Society's Child" released.

1967 — Leonard Bernstein's Inside Pop — The Rock Revolution. CBS-TV special showcases "Society's Child." Afterward, the controversial single about interracial love takes off. She releases her debut album at age 16 and receives the first of her nine Grammy nominations to date.

1968 — *The Secret Life of J. Eddy Fink* LP features guest Richie Havens.

1969 — Stars at Newport Folk Festival. Scores film *Four Rode Out* starring Leslie Nielsen, Pernell Roberts and Sue Lyon.

The 1970s

1973 — Roberta Flack scores a major hit with Ian's song "Jesse"; Dottie West, Chet Atkins, Joan Baez and many others record it.

1974 — Janis signs with Columbia Records and issues comeback LP *Stars*; Nina Simone, Mel Torme and others record its title tune.

1975 — "At Seventeen" becomes a smash hit; Grammy-nominated LP *Between the Lines* sells a million. Janis guests on the premiere broadcast of NBC's Saturday Night Live.

1976 — Grammy Award for "At Seventeen." Grammy Award for engineering *Between the Lines*. Hit album *Aftertones* features guest appearances by Odetta and Phoebe Snow, and spawns No. 1 hit in Japan, "Love Is Blind."

1977 — Sings and writes theme for the movie *Betrayal*. Sings harmony on Jean Ritchie LP *None But One*, named *Rolling Stone's* Folk Album of the Year.

1979 — Sings "Fly Too High" on soundtrack of the Jodie Foster movie *Foxes*. Album *Night Rains* features guests Clarence Clemons, Ron Carter & Chick Corea, plus theme from the Julie Harris film *The Bell Jar* and the U.K. hit "The Other Side of the Sun."

The 1980s

1980 — "Fly Too High" becomes international disco hit. Composes theme for the Chuck Connors/Glenn Ford film *Virus.*

1981 — Jazz vocal Grammy nomination for duet with Mel Torme "Silly Habits." Contributes six songs to ABC Movie of the Week *Freedom*, starring Mare Winningham. Janis is 30.

1982 — Children's music Grammy Award for *In Harmony 2*.

1987 — Kathy Mattea records Ian's song "Every Love" on her million selling *Untasted Honey* album. Jazz star Dianne Schuur records "Hearts Take Time." Writes songs for *"Murder She Wrote"* TV episode starring Charlie Daniels.

1988 — Moves to Nashville. Amy Grant sings Ian's "What About the Love" on her million-selling album *Lead Me On*.

1989 — Honored on VH-1's National Association of Songwriters show.

The 1990s

1990 — Bette Midler records Ian's song "Some People's Lives"; the album by that title goes on to sell two million copies.

1992 — Contributes "Days Like These" to the soundtrack of the John Mellencamp movie **Falling From Grace**.

1993 — Issues Grammy-nominated comeback album **Breaking Silence**. Becomes a popular guest on shock-jock Howard Stern's radio and TV broadcasts. Begins talking openly of her lesbianism. Nanci Griffith records "This Old Town" on her Grammy-winning album **Other Voices Other Rooms**.

1994 — John Mellencamp makes single & video of her song "All Roads to the River," from his **Human Wheels** album. Ian begins writing monthly column for **The Advocate**. Kathy Mattea records "Emmanuel" on Grammy-winning album **Good News**. Maura O'Connell sings Ian's "Every Love" at Ted Kennedy's wedding.

1995 — Issues album **Revenge**; nominated as pop album of the year at the Nashville Music Awards. PolyGram issues 42-song CD collection **Society's Child: The Anthology**. Janis begins writing column for **Performing Songwriter** magazine.

1997 — **Hunger** album for Windham Hill Records. Records "Emmanuel" with Deana Carter and Kathy Mattea for Windham Hill CD **The Carols of Christmas**.

1998 — Warner Bros. Publications issues retrospective songbook **The Songs of Janis Ian**.

GUITAR TAB GLOSSARY **

TABLATURE EXPLANATION

READING TABLATURE: Tablature illustrates the six strings of the guitar. Notes and chords are indicated by the placement of fret numbers on a given string(s).

String ⑥, 3rd Fret   String ① 12th Fret   A "C" Chord   C Chord Arpeggiated
String ③ 13th Fret

BENDING NOTES

HALF STEP: Play the note and bend string one half step.*

WHOLE STEP: Play the note and bend string one whole step.

WHOLE STEP AND A HALF: Play the note and bend string a whole step and a half.

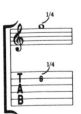

SLIGHT BEND (Microtone): Play the note and bend string slightly to the equivalent of half a fret.

PREBEND (Ghost Bend): Bend to the specified note, before the string is picked.

PREBEND AND RELEASE: Bend the string, play it, then release to the original note.

REVERSE BEND: Play the already-bent string, then immediately drop it down to the fretted note.

BEND AND RELEASE: Play the note and gradually bend to the next pitch, then release to the original note. Only the first note is attacked.

*A half step is the smallest interval in Western music; it is equal to one fret. A whole step equals two frets.

UNISON BEND: Play both notes and immediately bend the lower note to the same pitch as the higher note.

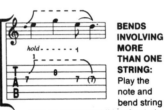

DOUBLE NOTE BEND: Play both notes and immediately bend both strings simultaneously.

BENDS INVOLVING MORE THAN ONE STRING: Play the note and bend string while playing an additional note (or notes) on another string(s). Upon release, relieve pressure from additional note(s), causing original note to sound alone.

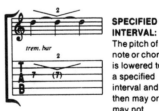

BENDS INVOLVING STATIONARY NOTES: Play notes and bend lower pitch, then hold until release begins (indicated at the point where line becomes solid).

TREMOLO BAR

SPECIFIED INTERVAL: The pitch of a note or chord is lowered to a specified interval and then may or may not return to the original pitch. The activity of the tremolo bar is graphically represented by peaks and valleys.

UN-SPECIFIED INTERVAL: The pitch of a note or a chord is lowered to an unspecified interval.

HARMONICS

NATURAL HARMONIC: A finger of the fret hand lightly touches the note or notes indicated in the tab and is played by the pick hand.

ARTIFICIAL HARMONIC: The first tab number is fretted, then the pick hand produces the harmonic by using a finger to lightly touch the same string at the second tab number (in parenthesis) and is then picked by another finger.

ARTIFICIAL "PINCH" HAR-MONIC: A note is fretted as indicated by the tab, then the pick hand produces the harmonic by squeezing the pick firmly while using the tip of the index finger in the pick attack. If parenthesis are found around the fretted note, it does not sound. No parenthesis means both the fretted note and A.H. are heard simultaneously.

© 1990 Beam Me Up Music
c/o CPP/Belwin, Inc. Miami, Florida 33014
International Copyright Secured   Made in U.S.A.   All Rights Reserved

**By Kenn Chipkin and Aaron Stang

RHYTHM SLASHES

STRUM INDICATIONS: Strum with indicated rhythm.
The chord voicings are found on the first page of the transcription underneath the song title.

INDICATING SINGLE NOTES USING RHYTHM SLASHES: Very often single notes are incorporated into a rhythm part. The note name is indicated above the rhythm slash with a fret number and a string indication.

ARTICULATIONS

HAMMER ON: Play lower note, then "hammer on" to higher note with another finger. Only the first note is attacked.

LEFT HAND HAMMER: Hammer on the first note played on each string with the left hand.

PULL OFF: Play higher note, then "pull off" to lower note with another finger. Only the first note is attacked.

FRET-BOARD TAPPING: "Tap" onto the note indicated by + with a finger of the pick hand, then pull off to the following note held by the fret hand.

TAP SLIDE: Same as fretboard tapping, but the tapped note is slid randomly up the fretboard, then pulled off to the following note.

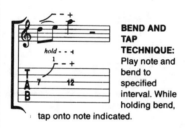

BEND AND TAP TECHNIQUE: Play note and bend to specified interval. While holding bend, tap onto note indicated.

LEGATO SLIDE: Play note and slide to the following note. (Only first note is attacked).

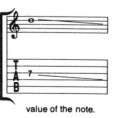

LONG GLISSANDO: Play note and slide in specified direction for the full value of the note.

SHORT GLISSANDO: Play note for its full value and slide in specified direction at the last possible moment.

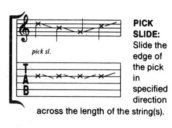

PICK SLIDE: Slide the edge of the pick in specified direction across the length of the string(s).

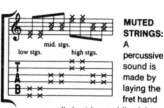

MUTED STRINGS: A percussive sound is made by laying the fret hand across all six strings while pick hand strikes specified area (low, mid, high strings).

PALM MUTE: The note or notes are muted by the palm of the pick hand by lightly touching the string(s) near the bridge.

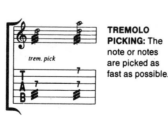

TREMOLO PICKING: The note or notes are picked as fast as possible.

TRILL: Hammer on and pull off consecutively and as fast as possible between the original note and the grace note.

ACCENT: Notes or chords are to be played with added emphasis.

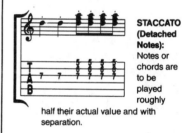

STACCATO (Detached Notes): Notes or chords are to be played roughly half their actual value and with separation.

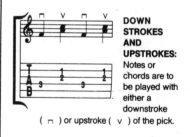

DOWN STROKES AND UPSTROKES: Notes or chords are to be played with either a downstroke (⊓) or upstroke (∨) of the pick.

VIBRATO: The pitch of a note is varied by a rapid shaking of the fret hand finger, wrist, and forearm.

Janis Ian   Hunger

Black & White
(Janis Ian)

On the Dark Side of Town
(Janis Ian)

Might As Well Be Monday
(Janis Ian)

Getting Over You
(Janis Ian/Gary Burr)

Searching for America
(Janis Ian)

Hunger
(Janis Ian)

Welcome to Acousticville
(Janis Ian)

Honor Them All
(Janis Ian)

Empty
(Janis Ian/Jim Varsos)

House Without A Heart
(Janis Ian)

Shadow
(Janis Ian)

Produced by Janis Ian & Jeff Balding
Searching for America produced by Ani Difranco

A Portion of the Proceeds will Benefit Futures for Children

...because Hunger starts in the Soul